The Master Arpeggio System for Jazz Improvisation II:
Minor & More

The Master Arpeggio System for Jazz Improvisation II: Minor & More
First Edition
Copyright © 2022 by Dennis Roberts

ISBN 978-1-7364821-9-3 (paperback)
ISBN 978-1-7364821-8-6 (ebook)

Formatting and cover design by Rachel Bostwick
Cover art: Md.Shafique Mahmud, designermdshafi at Fiverr

Printed in the United States

Published by MAS4JI.com
Bennington, VT

The Master Arpeggio System for Jazz Improvisation II: Minor & More

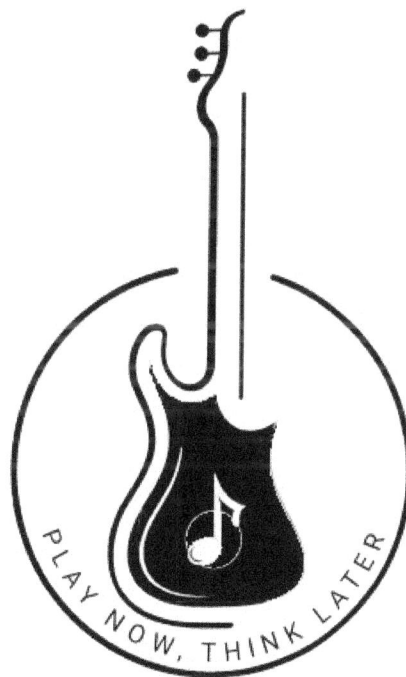

Dennis Roberts

PLAY NOW, THINK LATER

MAS4JI

For a link to download audio examples and for all correspondence, please contact the author at DRoberts@mas4ji.com or drrobts@gmail.com or look up MAS4JI or author's name on SoundCloud

Contents

Introduction

What to Expect

Welcome to the second book in the Master Arpeggio System for Jazz Improvisation series. MAS4JI II (my acronym for the long book title) is the companion to the first book, *The Master Arpeggio System for Jazz Improvisation* (MAS4JI). It builds on the foundation laid in that book and is, in effect, a continuation of the Master Arpeggio System program. Together, they present a more complete method for improvising great melodic lines for most jazz and fusion situations.

First, we'll learn just *five* new master arpeggios and develop those over the minor V–i and iiø–V–I chord progression, much like we did with the altered and major maps in the first book. We'll follow that up with *one* more new map—diminished—and learn how to use that over the V7b9 and #IV° chords, two common sounds that can be found in jazz. This will make a total of only *six* more master arpeggios that will vastly expand your growing arsenal of improvisational tools!

Next, we'll use *all* sixteen of our master arpeggios to navigate a variety of jazz turnarounds. This will prepare us for the grand finale of this book, where we'll apply *all* of our maps and techniques to solo over an intermediate jazz blues in our guitar-friendly key of A major.

In this book, I assume you're already familiar with MAS4JI and the content of the first book to avoid being too redundant so we can cover a lot of ground quickly. However, I still cover the first chapter thoroughly because it's very important and fundamental to the method, plus some musicians might join us her first and I have to bring them along too. Otherwise I try to keep moving along at a healthy pace.

I dedicate quality space to turnarounds and a jazz-blues solo to tie everything together and move us beyond simple lines. By the end of this book, you'll be ready for most of the common progressions you'll encounter in jazz standards and you should be able to form strategies for any variations you encounter.

Improvisation

Improvisation is the art of composing in the moment, creating melodic, musical lines on the fly. The Master Arpeggio System is a method that uses *chunking* and *key center* playing to help guitarists learn to improvise freely without a lot of overthinking by using triad and arpeggio-based lines and embellishing them with common devices used by all great jazz guitarists.

MAS4JI does *not* teach specific traditional jazz styles, although it's an *excellent* starting point for guitarists beginning to explore jazz because it introduces the fundamental concepts of consonance and dissonance and how to create and resolve tension while remaining melodic. It's a very visual system that teaches these ideas holistically, giving you the bigger picture rather than getting bogged down with in-depth study of music theory minutiae and endless, boring exercises and etudes.

Importantly, this is *not* where you turn to learn bebop, post-bop, hard bop or any other kind of bop. It doesn't teach swing, although you should be swinging those 8ths, a rhythmic move that will automatically begin to jazz up your lines from the very start. The Master Arpeggio System teaches you how to form lines and gives you a unique lens through which you can view anything else you learn moving forward in jazz and fusion because it uses techniques common to other jazz styles and genres and important relationships that underlie all jazz styles. It gives you a perspective on jazz fundamentals that will make moving into more academic waters much easier to manage.

Chunk It!

The two *key concepts* behind the Master Arpeggio System are a memorization technique called *chunking*, combined with *key center* playing. With chunking, we're taking a fairly large amount of detailed information and reducing to just a few bigger *chunks* of very useful information. As musicians, we're continually memorizing scales, triads, arpeggios, chords, progressions, and a host of other information. The Master Arpeggio System is an economical and helpful way of arranging some key elements of this information and using it to generate an endless variety of melodic lines.

Jazz standards—whether they're jazz-blues, the related Rhythm Changes, or more complex Coltrane changes—tend to move through shifting key centers in various patterns even though the song may generally be written in one key. We focus on the key centers instead of each individual chord. This is way we can *work smarter, not harder*. By simplifying things and forming good soloing strategies with the Master Arpeggio System, we can *play now and think later* applying this method to generate sophisticated lines with relative simplicity.

Who is This Book For?

MAS4JI is not for new guitarists, but for guitarists who've played for a couple years or more and who are familiar with basic ideas like major, minor, and pentatonic scales, intervals, and chord progressions, along with the ideas of triads and arpeggios. It's a great tool for guitarists from other genres who want to explore general jazz sounds to use in their own styles of playing, whether blues, rock, metal, progressive or jam band.

It's for self-taught, self-motivated guitarists who want to continue to develop their playing without formal education or to prepare for formal education. It helps you very clearly see the relationships between the elements of music that are used to create and resolve tension. The result is you can more easily see those connections when you move into deeper studies, giving you a distinct advantage in that regard.

It's a great quick-start method for guitarists who are moving into jazz and want a great overview of ideas they'll be studying and using, but without all the deeper academic vernacular and endless non-musical exercises. It's also a great method for students who need to improvise solos for recitals because it'll get your fingers walking along the fretboard quicker than most other available methods.

Remember: the music came first and all the theory came along later as a way to describe what's happening. With MAS4JI, you can learn *how* to do it and then learn all the labels and how to analyze it later if you desire. We just focus on *doing* it so you can enjoy playing with these ideas sooner and with more confidence. By the time you study the theory, you'll feel like you're just reviewing and labeling material you already know. I give you enough basic information to work with indefinitely and I put certain words in *italics* so you can research them further if you like.

Finally, MAS4JI is a great method for guitar teachers to use with students who want to learn to play jazz and solo with melodic, jazz-style phrasing. Once the instructor learns the Master Arpeggio concept, it's easily adaptable and can be used to effectively teach more traditional jazz styles in a way that students can readily grasp and apply in their own playing. It's a great way to introduce and demonstrate theory and techniques for more specific styles in a manner that's helpful and easier for students to understand.

In short, MAS4JI is for the curious and the musically adventurous who want to see musical ideas from a new perspective.

Get the Most Out of This Book

As with the first book, I recommend you study the book in chronological order, page by page and chapter by chapter, and don't skip around. It's a very progressive method where each new approach builds on the ones that came before it in a very logical way. It's not an abstract concept or approach, but a distinct method with definable parameters that move along step by step, much like a course that would be taught in a classroom setting or with an instructor.

The notation and tablature examples demonstrate the ideas being taught and generally keep things relatively simple, but I also combine the new ideas with the previous ones so they develop into lines you would ultimately be using in your actual playing, lines that use *all* the techniques freely at will. I do throw in a more complex line occasionally just to keep us all on our toes.

I encourage you to explore all the ideas on your own because MAS4JI is not a book of licks and phrases, it's a method that teaches you to create your own and the lines within are merely examples of the ideas being applied as an aid. If you stick to the master arpeggios and play *from* them, you will automatically generate strong, melodic lines, and the embellishments will fit together like flexible puzzle pieces that allow you to create any picture you want musically as things click and you have a few revealing "Aha!" moments and begin merging it with your own pre-existing playing style.

I hope you enjoy the book and that MAS4JI gives you a new perspective on improvisation and inspires new ideas and creativity that enhances your playing and takes you to new places.

Chapter One: A Minor Thing

First, a Few Notes

The first book, *The Master Arpeggio System for Jazz Improvisation*, introduced the major and altered master arpeggios in the key of A major with a focus on the major ii-V-I progression that's as common to jazz standards as the I-IV-V is to blues. I chose a very guitar-friendly key and stuck with it throughout to keep things very simple and direct so we could progressively build our ideas in a more linear fashion. I kept the tempos modest and limited the majority of the lines to 8th notes and triplets, only throwing in a few 16th notes for good measure.

In the same way, this book will pick right up with using the relative minor to A major—F# minor—to help us address playing over the minor key iiø-V-i. By doing this, anyone who has worked through the first book will *only* have five new master arpeggios (which I will again refer to as *maps* for short). The great thing is, there's only a *one note difference* in the new maps, so the learning curve is going to be considerably easier. Adding the diminished map will give us only *six* new maps to learn in MAS4JI II.

What is a Master Arpeggio?

To quickly recap, the master arpeggio is a comprehensive arpeggio that has one form when ascending and a different form when descending. Together, they comprise the complete master arpeggio form. The master arpeggio contains all of the triads and arpeggios we'll need for any given key and we'll learn some simple ways to extract what we need without practicing tons of boring exercises that require playing sets triads and arpeggios in root positions and inversions in all keys off of every note in a given scale. Our goal is to bypass most that work or to bring a different perspective to those of us who've already done that tedious work.

This chapter lays the foundation for everything we'll use in the chapters that follow. It's the brunt of our learning curve, after which things will get much easier and much more fun as we move into playing. This is where we calibrate our GPS so we can learn to navigate in the minor key neighborhood and, very soon, through the shifting keys of jazz blues.

Connecting the Dots:

Playing our Master Arpeggios

The fretboard diagram below is laid out in the standard format. The horizontal lines represent the strings. The bottom is the low E and the top is the high E. The vertical lines are frets and the number for the fret locations are labeled above the diagram. The black and white dots represent the notes we'll play on the guitar neck.

To play the minor master arpeggio, first play the black dots ascending from the sixth string to the first string and then play the white dots descending from the first string back down to the sixth string. Voila! You have played through the F# minor map.

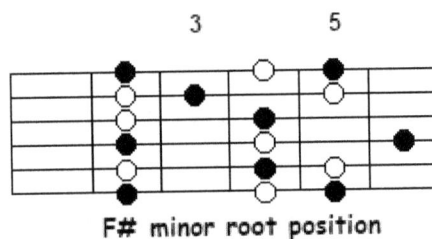

F# minor root position

Example 1 demonstrates playing our F#m map ascending and descending. But that's not the only way we need to be able to play this. We have to be able to play it *every which way*: frontward, backward, up, down, and inside out. Examples 2-4 give us some other ways to practice our minor map so we can thoroughly learn it. We need to get very comfortable with playing this.

1 Ascending Descending

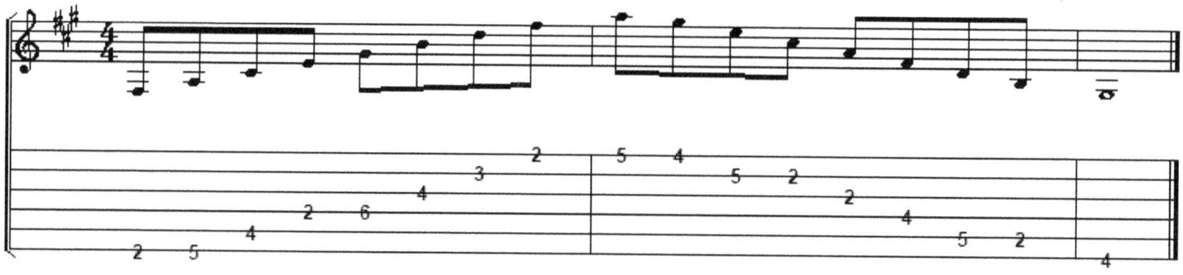

2 Also play . . .

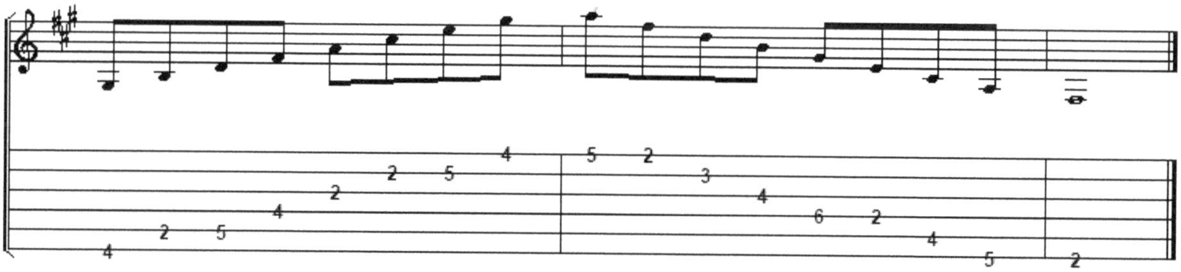

3 Then . . .

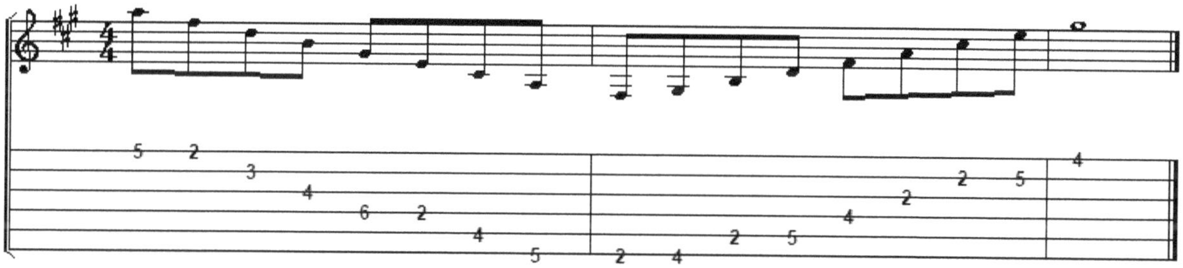

4 And . . .

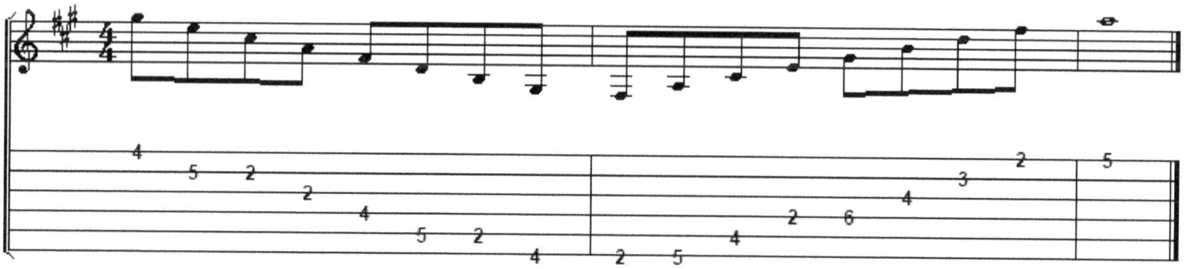

Smaller Chunks at First

Sometimes it helps to break the maps into smaller chunks to better facilitate learning them. The idea is to play through the *entire* map while *feeling* these smaller shapes under your fingers. Get the feel for each set of three strings but play through them all without pausing. If it helps, think in sets of three strings while memorizing the entire map.

The following fretboard diagrams demonstrate how we can mentally divide our first master arpeggio to make it easier to learn. Likewise, Example 5 demonstrates how we can think of these partial maps as we play through them and get the feel for the larger map under our fingers. What is also very helpful is that the other maps we'll be learning use some of the same forms or very similar forms, so we'll see repetitive patterns throughout.

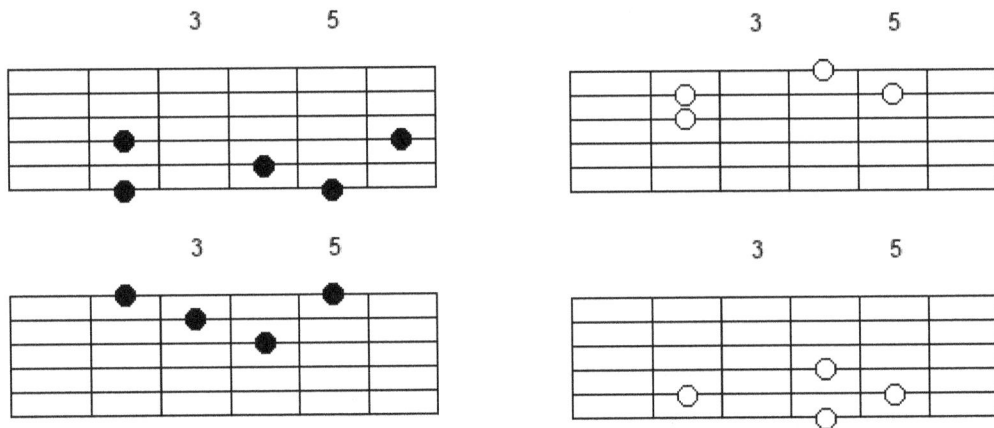

Smaller chunks

Remember to use this as a memory *aid* and not as a *crutch* because we're going to need to be able to very freely dissect these arpeggios into smaller pieces from any point within and that's *much* easier to do if we keep our focus on the bigger picture, namely the complete minor map.

Also, this gives us *only* ten maps we'll need for our minor key playing, five of which we already know because they're the *same* as the major maps we learned in the first book. Additionally, there's only a *one-note* difference in the other five maps, so the learning curve is greatly reduced. It's going to be so much easier learning only *five* new maps rather than lots of smaller triads and arpeggios like many of us have done while taking the traditional learning route. We don't need that here!

Learning the Maps

To begin, let's learn five F# minor maps and pair them with five F# harmonic minor maps. As we learn them, take note of where the one-note difference is. This one note offsets things just enough to give us some different sounds, which we'll learn to use in the following chapters.

My recommendation is playing each new map using the methods from Examples 1 through 4, breaking them into smaller chunks as needed until we can ditch those training wheels, which should be pretty quickly. As soon as you're comfortable, start playing up one map and down another. For example, play black dots of the F# minor map ascending, followed by the white dots of the F# harmonic minor map descending, as demonstrated in Example 6. Then play them the opposite way, like in Example 7.

6 F# minor   F# harmonic minor

7 F# minor   F# harmonic minor

Here are some ways to learn and practice the maps as pairs to help memorize them and prepare for playing them in *all* directions so we'll be versatile with them:

- Play the F# minor map ascending black dots and F# harmonic minor map descending white dots
- Play the F# minor map ascending white dots and F# harmonic minor map descending black dots
- Play the F# minor map descending black dots and F# harmonic minor map ascending white dots
- Play the F# minor map descending white dots and F# harmonic minor map ascending black dots
- Do the same four exercises starting with the F# harmonic minor map and finishing with the F# minor map

I'm *not* a big fan of exercises, but practicing this way at first is part of the learning and memorizing process. This is the most structured the practice will be and the learning curve will be remarkably quick for anyone who has

already learned the major maps and the one-note difference for the har--
monic minor map will further speed up the process.

Presenting: The Minor Master Arpeggio Pairs

F# minor root position

F# harmonic minor

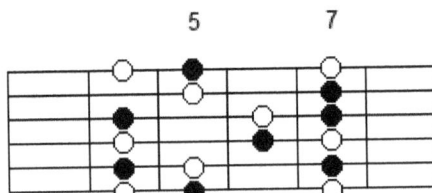

F# minor from 2nd

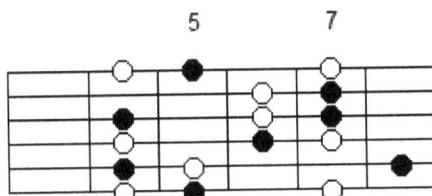

F# harmonic minor

10

11

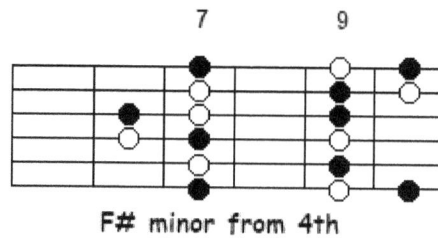

F# minor from 4th

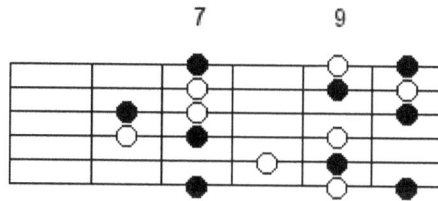

F# harmonic minor

12

13

15

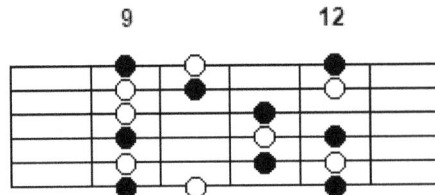

F# minor from 5th

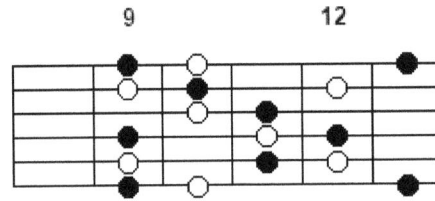

F# harmonic minor

14

15

F# minor from b7th

F# harmonic minor

The Final Step

No more playing through the maps with predictable patterns. Those were a means to an end for memorizing them. The goal now is to play more randomly, moving through black dots in smaller groups, ascending or descending for three, four, five, or even six notes, switching to the *nearest* white dot above or below and either changing direction or continuing in the

17

same direction. You can pivot off of black or white dots and play up and down (or down and up) through a small group of the same black or white dots like you would when playing standard arpeggios. You'll even recognize many of your familiar triads and arpeggios nestled within the master arpeggios; incorporate this knowledge immediately!

This is a great thing to do mindlessly while watching TV, although I also recommended doing some focused practice as well to speed up the process. Both are helpful because the "mindless" practice teaches your fingers to walk freely when you're distracted, more subconsciously and without effort, while the mindful practice is much more deliberate and directed.

Don't play through Examples 18 or 19 (*once* is okay, just to get the idea). They're just guides, demonstrating playing through the maps randomly, switching between black and white dots every which way, frontward, backward, up and down and inside out, from any point to any point, freely and without restrictions. This helps us to lay a strong foundation and framework we can use to throw together melodic lines without hardly even thinking.

Example 18 demonstrates random movement using only the F# minor map, while Example 19 demonstrates random movement between the F# minor and F# harmonic minor maps, one of our major goals. The great thing about this is that, with a little time and effort, the first map will connect to the second map, which will in turn connect to the one above it until the maps are intertwined like a chain link fence. Soon we will begin seeing the fretboard as one giant master arpeggio we can move through freely. This is possible because we've chunked our information into fewer units so it then becomes easier to chunk into one large map that covers the entire fingerboard.

18

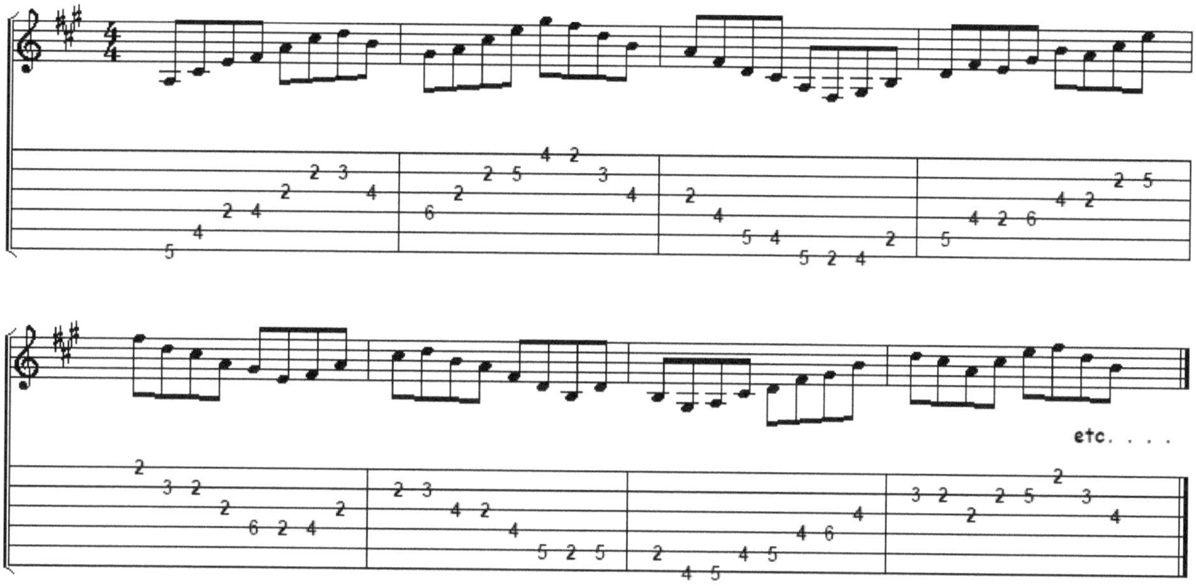

19

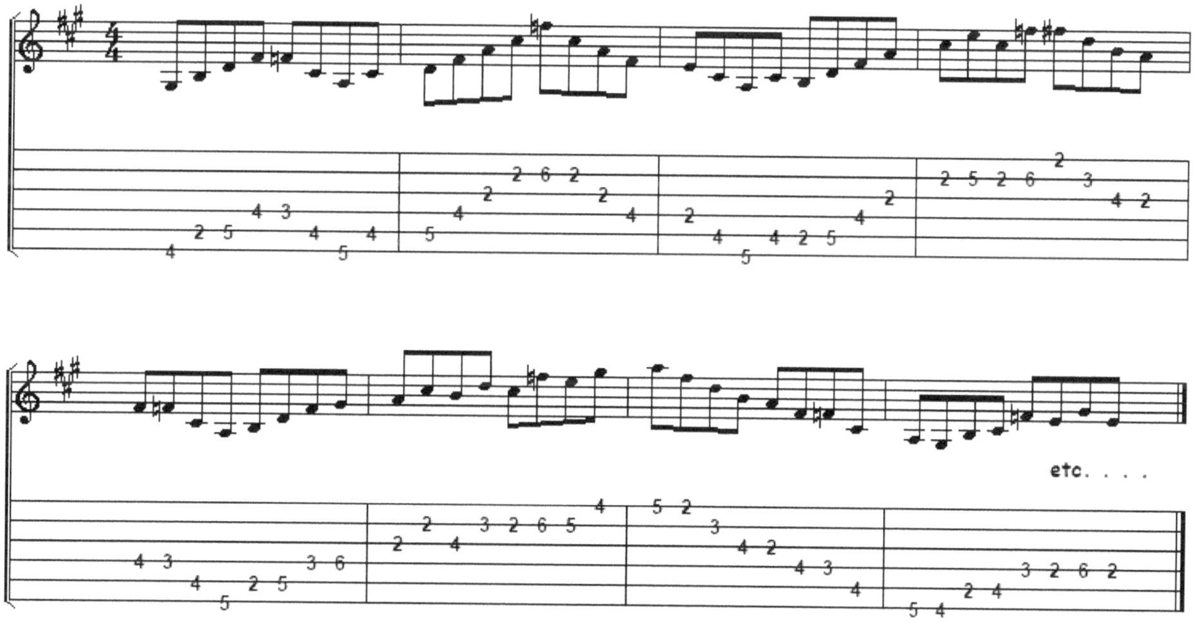

Chapter Two: Line Dancing

Tension and Resolution

Improvising lines in jazz is about creating and resolving tension. It's about the constant interplay of consonance and dissonance locked in a continuous dance where we choreograph all the moves. We are the director, storyteller, composer, and creative force that propels the music forward with our solos as we create and resolve tension

We're going to explore the V–i and iiø–V–i progressions. While songs in minor keys are not as common in jazz as major keys, these sounds *are* frequent key centers in various substitutes and turnarounds, so it's very helpful to understand how to navigate them. The V7 and iiø–V7 are used to create tension and that's where we'll use the F# harmonic minor maps. We'll use our F# minor maps to resolve that tension.

We're going to apply our same ten steps to progressively develop our lines by embellishing and manipulating the minor maps. Because these maps are easier to learn and apply, I'll move fairly quickly so we can focus more on applying *all* of our maps to turnarounds and a solo to tie everything together and put it in a real world context.

Get a Little Loopy

I recommend practicing with a looper pedal. They're included in most multi-effects and they're even available in inexpensive mini pedals. A drum and looper pedal is even better, especially if there are some jazz rhythm options available. It's very helpful to record a simple one chord *vamp*, like an F#m7 and play both maps over it, then doing the same with a C#7 chord vamp, listening what sounds good and what doesn't. What doesn't sound as good is where you're creating tension and what sounds better is the resolution. Sometimes it's easier to hear over just one chord because they'll sound better over their respective chords when we create cohesive lines.

Follow this with the very important V7–i progression: C#7–F#m7. Playing the F# harmonic minor over the C#7 is the exotic *Phrygian dominant* sound that's common to a lot of heavy metal and neo-classical music, most notably exemplified in the playing of Yngwie Malmsteen. It's also a cornerstone of Flamenco music and is the instantly recognizable sound of the classic jazz standard *Caravan* by Duke Ellington. It has been extensively used by Al Di Meola and John McLaughlin and is also used for some Middle Eastern sounds. Practicing playing over looped progressions helps us get the sounds in our ears so we can begin building an arsenal of ideas for future improvisation.

Let's Dance

First, let's form our most basic lines using just the first two master arpeggios together, starting in the first position around the second fret. We'll play them much the same way we did when doing our random practice, but now we're going to switch between the two maps over the corresponding chords while always trying to be musical. We're going to play phrases instead of random bits and pieces. By now, we should be slicing and dicing those two maps and tossing them together like a Chef Salad full of tasty morsels that will give us a nice variety of flavors as we move forward.

The following examples are very basic, melodic lines formed by nothing more than simply connecting the basic maps over their respective chords. This is the core of all great lines and *everything* that follows are merely ways of manipulating and embellishing the basic maps for more sophisticated and interesting sounds.

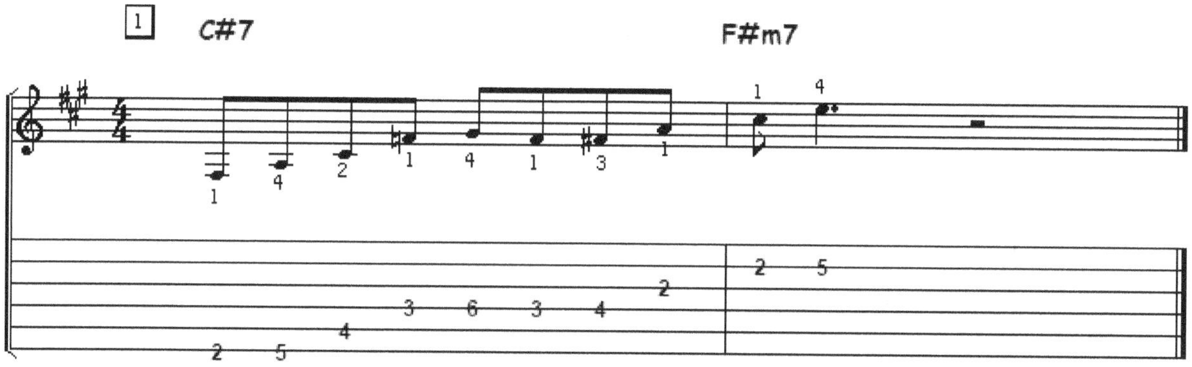
1
C#7
F#m7

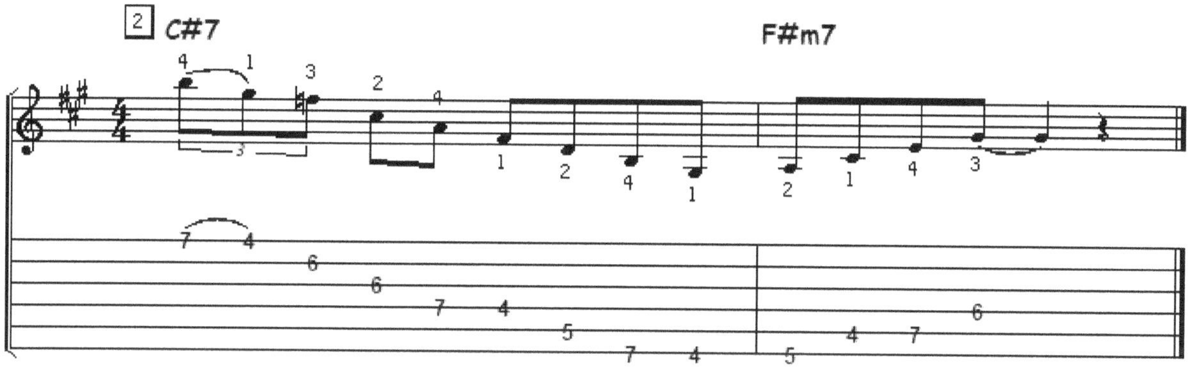
2
C#7
F#m7

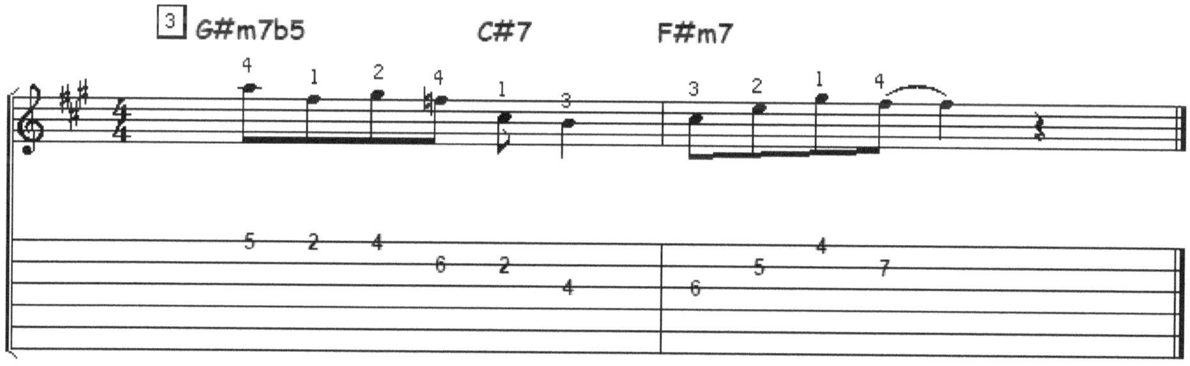
3
G#m7b5
C#7
F#m7

Out of Order

The first way we'll change up our lines for variation is to play the notes of any portion of the maps out of order, creating *permutations*. Below is a diagram of the first four notes of the minor map followed by Example 4, which demonstrates how we play permutations. Don't turn this into an exercise because there are *way too many* variations for all the maps in all keys with different numbers of notes, from triads on up. Just familiarize yourself with the idea and, armed with the knowledge you can do this while playing . . . play! Just start using this idea in your phrasing and you'll find it comes very easily.

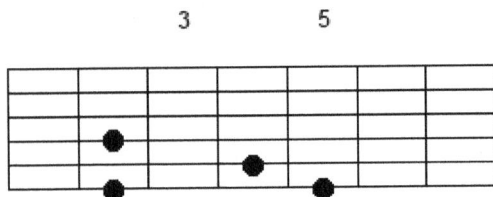

4 Permutations   etc. . . . .

Here are a couple lines demonstrating playing notes out of order. It's easiest to start off using these with groups of three or four notes from the maps. Pretty quickly, you'll find you can break your maps up all over the place so you play more *angular* lines that become increasingly intervallic in nature, a very simple but key technique used in modern playing by all great guitarists in jazz and fusion. Don't overthink it, just *do* it.

It's Okay to Skip!

Yup! Sometimes we walk, sometimes we run, and sometimes we skip! Don't worry, you won't look silly skipping notes and it'll make your lines sound more interesting and give you more variations for cool, melodic phrasing.

Here's our first position F# minor map, followed by the map shown only on the bottom three strings. Example 7 shows how we get some interesting new sounds by simply skipping a black or white dot when playing our maps. Now we can play our maps out of order *and* skip some too. How fortuitous!

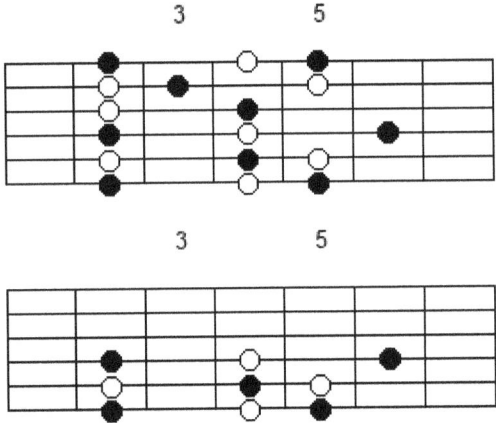

Here are a couple of simple lines demonstrating that, yes, it's definitely okay to skip. Try it, you'll like it!

Black and White

Playing in black and white really opens things up. We play in black and white when we play our black and white dots *consecutively*, one note after another, adding a scalar aspect to our maps. It breaks up our maps very nicely and gives us an infinite variety of options. As we progress, we will increasingly blur the lines between playing maps and playing in black and white, although it's helpful to *always* play from the perspective of our maps.

The diagram below again displays our F# minor map on the lower three strings and the examples that follow demonstrate playing up a portion of our map and back down with *all* the black and white dots consecutively, then playing down a portion of our map and up with the black and white dots together. So this is really just another way we connect the dots.

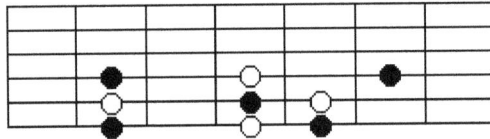

10

11

Here's an example of this idea in action.

12   *G#m7b5*   *C#7*   *F#m7*

Harmonic Minor Focal Point

Did you notice that *gap*? There's a gap between a couple of the notes in the harmonic minor scale. Because there's only a one-note difference between this map and the minor map, I'm now going to focus specifically on the area of the harmonic minor map that gives it its signature sound when playing in black and white. Sometimes we want to capitalize on this sound and bring it out, while at others we'll want to downplay it, which we'll learn to do later.

The diagram below displays the F# harmonic minor map, followed by the areas of the map that give it a distinct sound, then Example 13 demonstrates this more exotic sound in black and white.

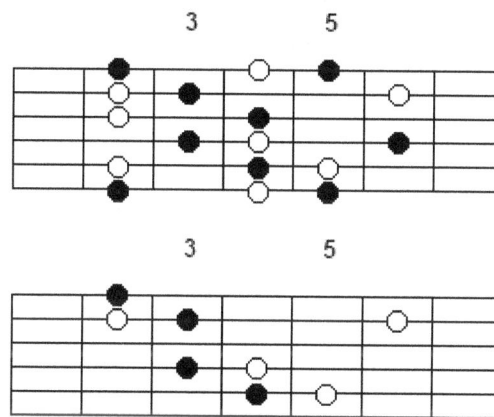

Examples 14 and 15 demonstrate a couple of lines that express the exotic sounds available within our harmonic minor map when we play in black and white. For the more theory-minded out there, the sound of the harmonic minor over the V7 (C#7 chord here) is the Phrygian dominant, i.e. C# Phrygian dominant, while over the iim7b5 (G#m7b5 below), the sound is a Locrian with a natural 6 (G# Locrian natural 6 or Locrian 6). They're derived from the parent F# melodic minor.

This chapter represents the simplest and most direct ways we can use the minor and harmonic minor map to efficiently improvise melodic lines. Now, let's look at some more ways we can use our maps to give us new choices and more variety for creative phrasing.

Chapter Three:
Use the Fourths

Musicians like Herbie Hancock and McCoy Tyner really got the ball rolling and set the stage for the modern use of fourths intervals in contemporary jazz playing. Now they're everywhere!

To play fourths, we play *across* adjacent strings, often at the same fret. For the minor map, the only different fourth is the *augmented* fourth interval, also known as the *flat* or *diminished* fifth. However, the harmonic minor map is a little trickier because there's a flatted fourth that looks like a major third in addition to the augmented fourth.

The diagrams below demonstrate the fourths across strings for the first position of the minor map followed by the fourths for the harmonic minor map. Notice the augmented and flat fourth intervals and learn where they are in each position as you explore the sound in your own improvisations. Yes, it's a little tricky! ... But you can break the rules. You can just continue on in fourths in the next octave or play *faux* fourths; fourths that wouldn't appear naturally in the properly *harmonized* scale. Just remember: if it *sounds* good it *is* good. Make music!

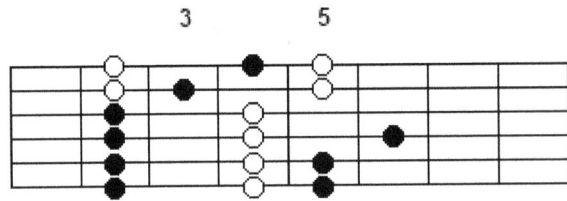

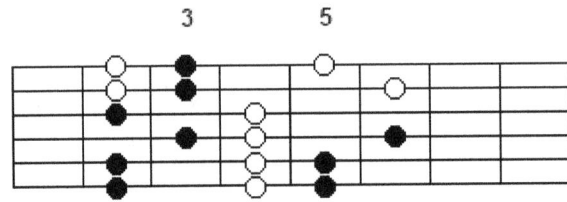

Now that we took care of that, let's use our fourths of habit in a couple of lines

3/4 + 4/3 = Creating Fractions in Your Playing?!

The next step is combining thirds (what we're naturally playing when using all black or all white dots) with the fourths. We can play a third interval followed by a fourth interval or—wait for it—a fourth interval followed by a third interval. Of course, we can precede or follow with more third or fourth intervals because there aren't any strict rules that apply to this simple concept. Also, these give us various inversions of the triads and arpeggios embedded in our maps without *any* tedious exercises, just a temporary shift in our thinking and taking a different path through our maps, as our next diagrams and examples will demonstrate. Example 5 demonstrates this in the minor map and Example 6 for the harmonic minor map.

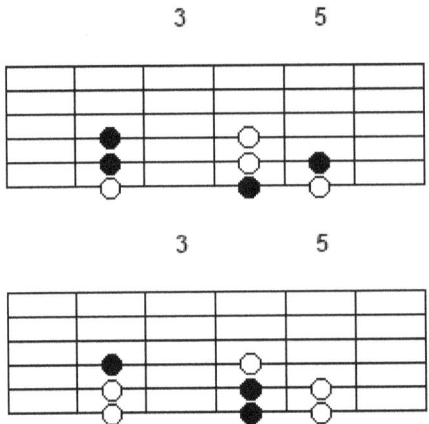

5   a)   b)

6   a)   b)

NOTE: the small dots are the other notes of the map and are just for context.

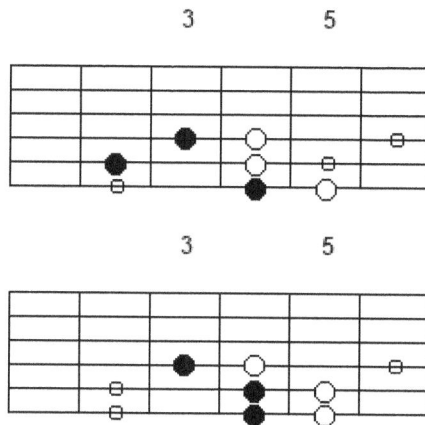

3   5

3   5

6 a)   b)

And now it's time to play a couple lines that use these combinations of intervals conveniently lurking within our maps.

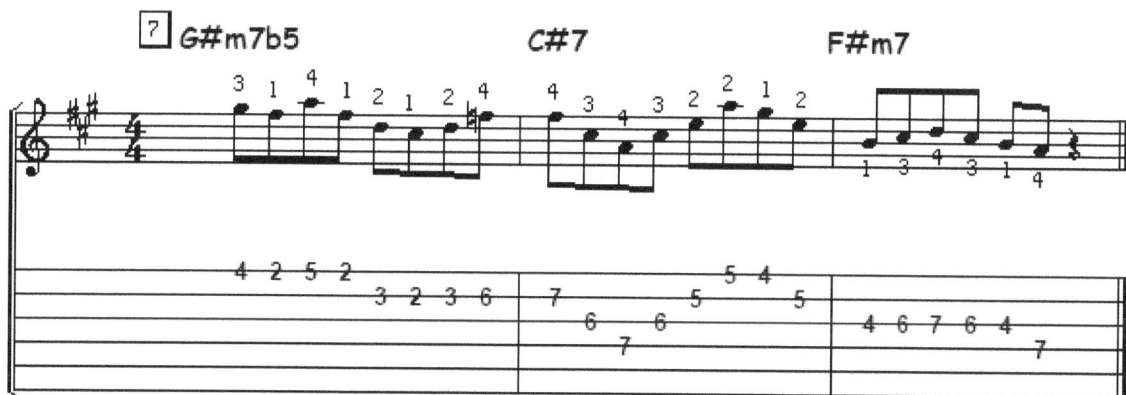

7 G#m7b5   C#7   F#m7

The one guitarist that most prominently comes to mind when I think of playing in thirds and fourths with incredible proficiency and efficiency is none other than the *Thunder from Down Under*, Frank Gambale. Fourths, thirds, and their combinations present excellent opportunities for sweep and economy picking at higher speeds. Example 8 is my personal application of these ideas for a line inspired by the master picker.

This last one is nice because it uses a different area of the fretboard than many of the previous examples and it uses a wide variety of the ideas we've been exploring (and I even snuck one in that we'll cover later).

One of the *main* differences between jazz and fusion is that, to make your lines sound jazzier you want to *swing* your 8ths, giving your lines that certain *lilt* that automatically gives you the jazz vibe. Fusion lines generally use more straight 8ths, playing more squarely *on the beat*, much like a rock player, although you can move between swinging your 8ths and playing them straight according to your personal tastes as you develop your style using these ideas. Both sound great and bring variety to your lines.

Chapter Four:
Powerful Pentatonic

Within each minor map are *three* pentatonic scales that we can tap into when improvising melodic lines and they also give us opportunities to use our arsenal of pentatonic blues licks. Use them *all* because they're powerful tools for melodic phrasing. Again, swing the rhythm a little and you're already in jazz territory. You can even shuffle a little; it's your call (and response).

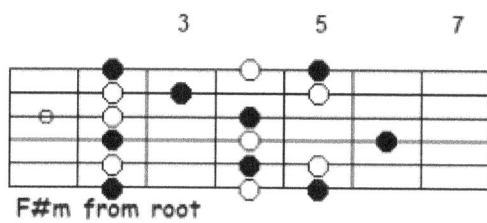

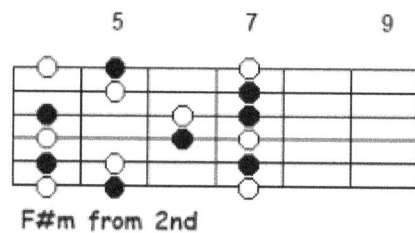

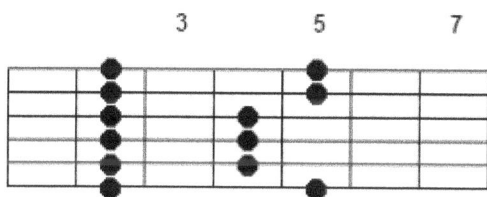

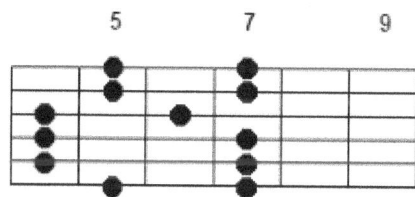

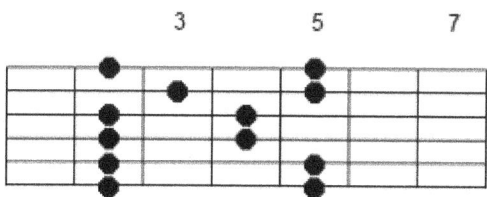

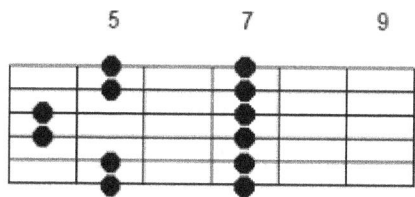

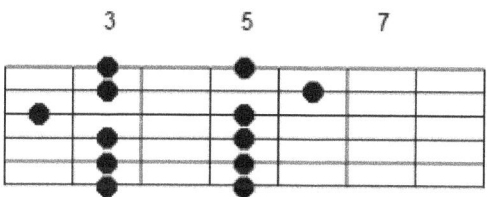

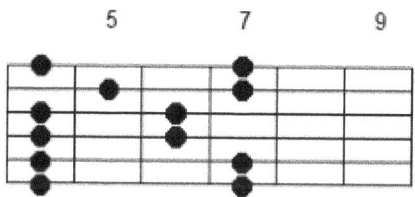

F#m from root

F#m from 2nd

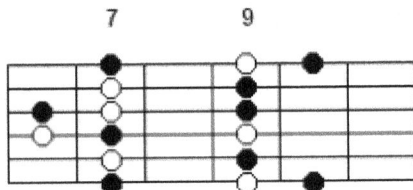

F#m from b3rd

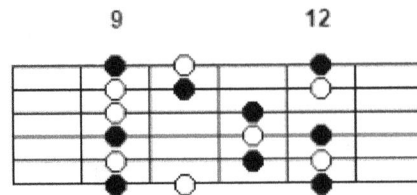

F#m from 5th

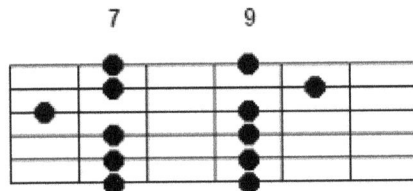

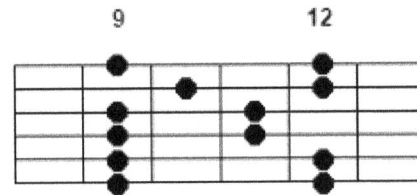

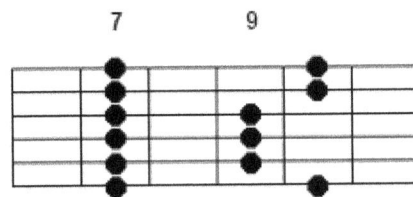

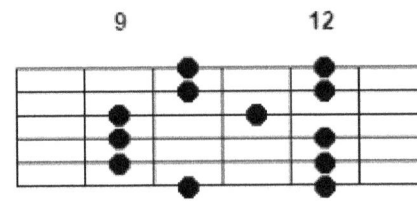

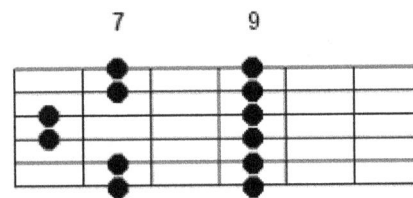

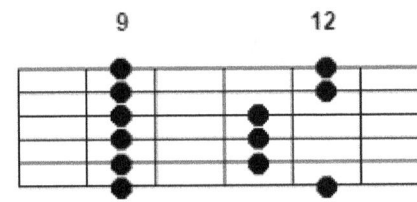

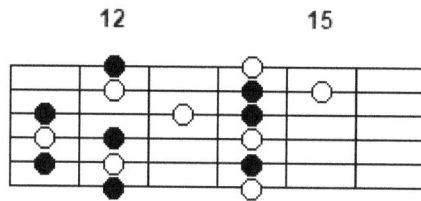

F#m from b7

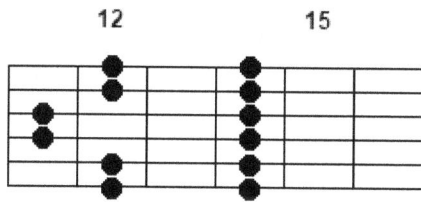

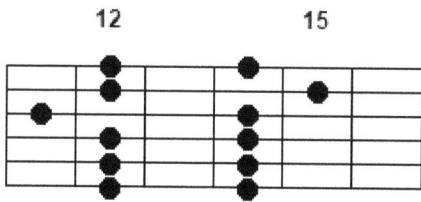

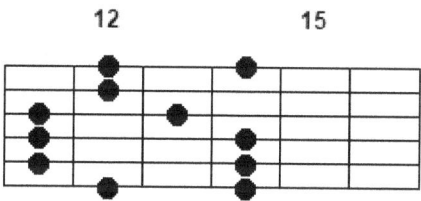

Now, let's put these into practice

An Exotic Pentatonic

What if we want to use a bluesy sound over the V7 chord but still retain its cool, exotic flavor? The harmonic minor map doesn't contain any of our familiar pentatonic scales, but we can find the one that *almost* fits and then change the one crucial note that defines that unique sound and form a nice exotic pentatonic variation that works great for playing some interesting off-blues lines.

The following diagrams display the harmonic minor map, followed first by the pentatonic scale that closely fits with it, then the alteration that keeps that one-note difference intact so we can keep the distinct flavor of the harmonic minor map. Now we can play some mildly exotic near-blues. Technically, you could even move between the pentatonic and the exotic pentatonic to mix things up a little.

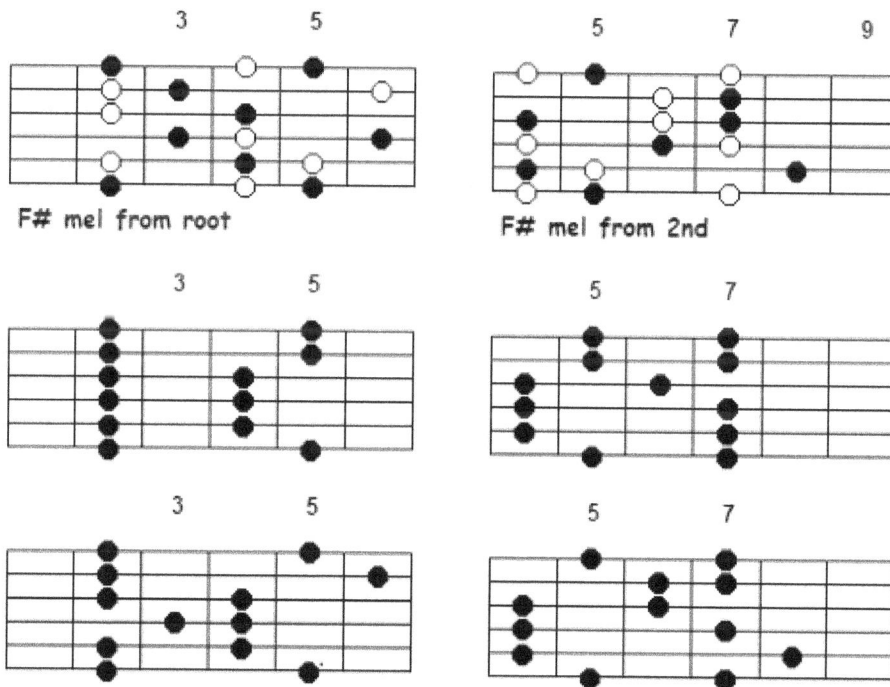

F# mel from root

F# mel from 2nd

43

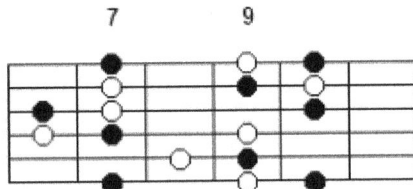

F# mel from 4th

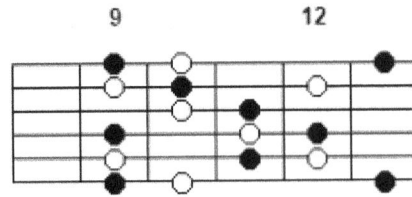

F# mel from 5th

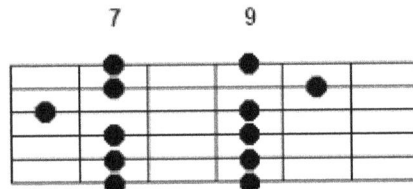

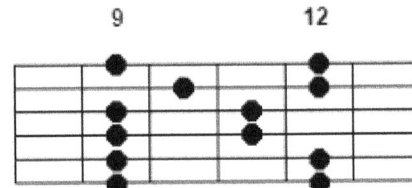

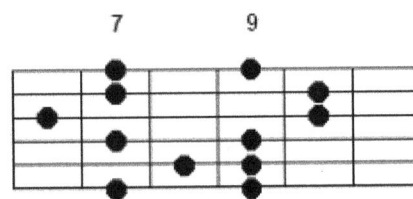

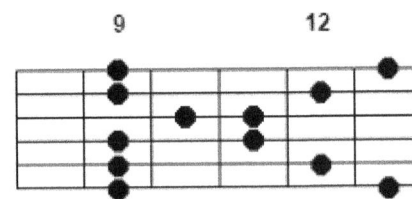

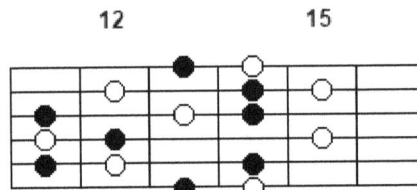

F# mel from 7th

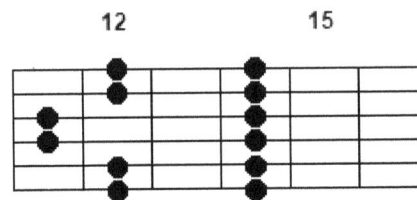

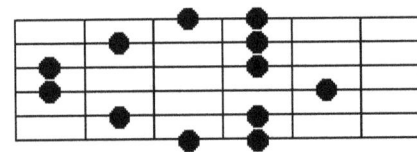

44

Examples 4 through 6 explore our exotic pentatonic for some slightly off-blues lines.

Chapter Five:
A Minor Chromaddict

Chromaticism is, it seems, the *heart* of jazz and fusion lines. Chromatic notes are the adornment that color the lines like nothing else can. With chromaticism, *all* twelve notes become fair game. Of course, we don't just play all twelve notes willy-nilly like some kind of crazy person, some mad musical scientist creating monsters in his (or her) laboratory.

There's a method to this madness called chromaticism and we're going to examine three of the main techniques for using it. After all, chromaticism is what we've been working toward all this time. It's the cherry on top of the sundae. However, before we could go crazy with chromaticism, we had to lay a foundation for keeping things melodic so we have something solid to build on. But now we're ready!

Approach Tones

Approach tones are a very simple concept that can drastically affect our lines. A well-placed approach tone can work wonders for adding jazz flair and style. Our diagram below takes a small portion of our minor map in the first position, black dots only, and throws a chromatic approach tone in, represented by a white dot. Example 1 demonstrates one way we could play this (there are others). The approach tone is circled in the music notation and a + above the tablature.

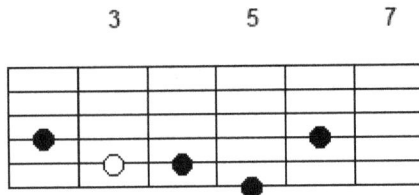

1 F#m7

Example 2 and 3 demonstrate modest use of an approach tone. Notice how one well-placed approach tone can affect a line. It has a distinctly jazzier quality. Of course, we can go pretty crazy with approach tones if we want. It's not a crime . . . unless you put one under a rest (I'll see myself out).

2 *C#7*   *F#m7*

3 *G#m7b5*   *C#7*   *F#m7*

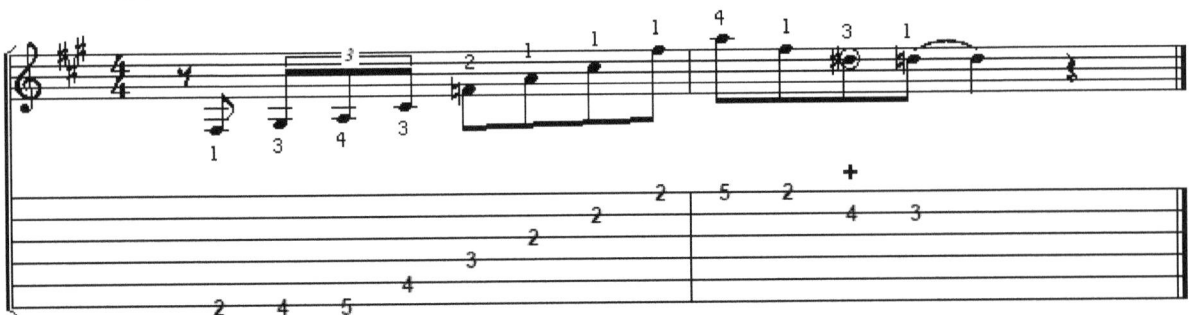

The Passing Tone

Now we're going to kick things up a notch! A passing tone is a *non-diatonic* note that is placed in between *any* two diatonic notes from the map when we're playing in black and white, i.e. scalar. Not only do you hear this all the time in traditional jazz and bebop, it's also a definitive mainstay of fusion and is prevalent in the modern rock-fusion playing of guitarists like Steve Morse, Greg Howe, Brett Garsed, Richie Kotzen, Buckethead, Tom Quayle, and pretty much everyone.

The next diagram shows a passing tone placed between two notes in the minor map, just one of the many places where we can use them. Basically, you can put a passing tone *anywhere* there's not a note (or dot} in our map diagrams. You can use them sparingly or really go crazy with them. You can use them here and there. You can use them *anywhere*.

Example 4 puts the passing tone in context.

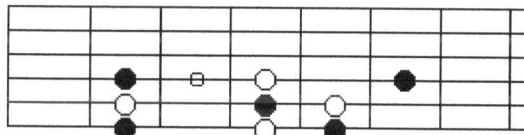

4 F#m7

49

Examples 5 through 7 place passing tones in our lines, combining the maps with more black and white playing. The circled notes on the notation staff indicate the chromatic notes. Some are passing tones and some are approach tones. Mixing them up is a great way to start disguising the direct exotic sound of the harmonic minor and to break up the maps more. Really great jazz and fusion playing is a strong balance of scalar lines mixed with triads, arpeggios, chromaticism, and all the techniques and ideas we're learning here.

When playing all these lines that use more black and white scalar playing mixed with chromaticism, try to *always* play from the perspective of the maps. I'm *always* playing the maps and not scales. Everything embellishes the maps and the embellishments are simply becoming increasingly elaborate and numerous as I blur the lines between the two and bleed them together. Starting from the maps helps me see my resolutions to target tones and keeps my lines melodic.

Chromatic Enclosures

Our final chromatic embellishment was very popular in the bebop era but has been used in classical music and continues to be in use today. Guitarists Pat Metheny and Mike Stern are exemplary in their creative modern application of these (along with the other chromatic ornaments we've just learned). There's something about chromatic enclosures that harkens back to more traditional jazz sounds, but they can also be used very effectively in modern lines.

Essentially, chromatic enclosures surround a diatonic note before landing on it and they contain a mix of both diatonic and non-diatonic notes. Sometimes they even hit the note and then come back to land on it. You can enclose a diatonic note with just two notes, with three notes, four, or even five notes.

You can play them in a variety of different ways, using one or two strings. The next diagram shows our diatonic notes in black and the two chromatic notes I'll use to demonstrate our enclosures in white. Example 8 will show some very common ways we would target a note using them. The last note in the bracket is the targeted tone.

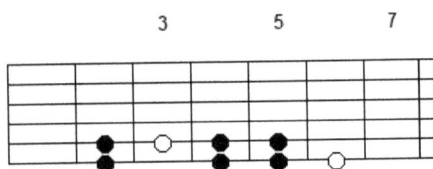

The final examples for this chapter are going to use various enclosures, which are highlighted, but I'm also going to use the approach tones and passing tones too for very realistic lines that a jazz and fusion guitarist could play, freely mixing the maps with black and white playing. The last note in each bracket is the targeted tone.

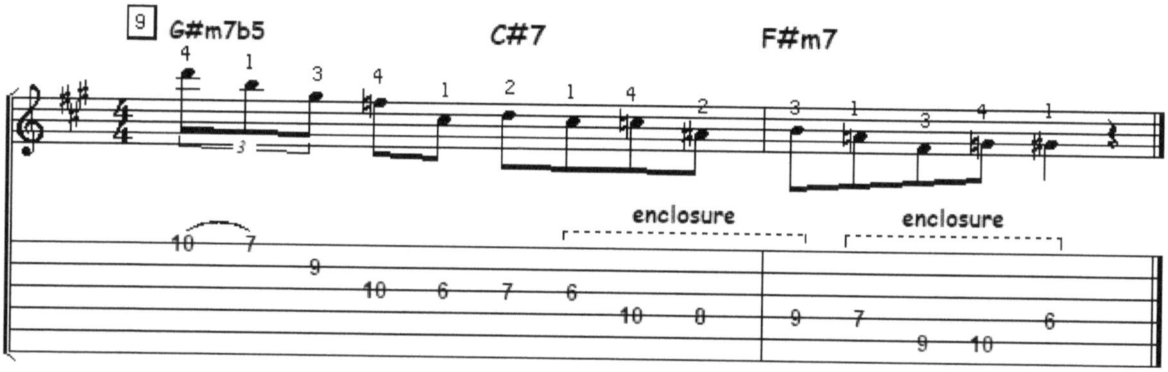
9
G#m7b5
C#7
F#m7
enclosure
enclosure

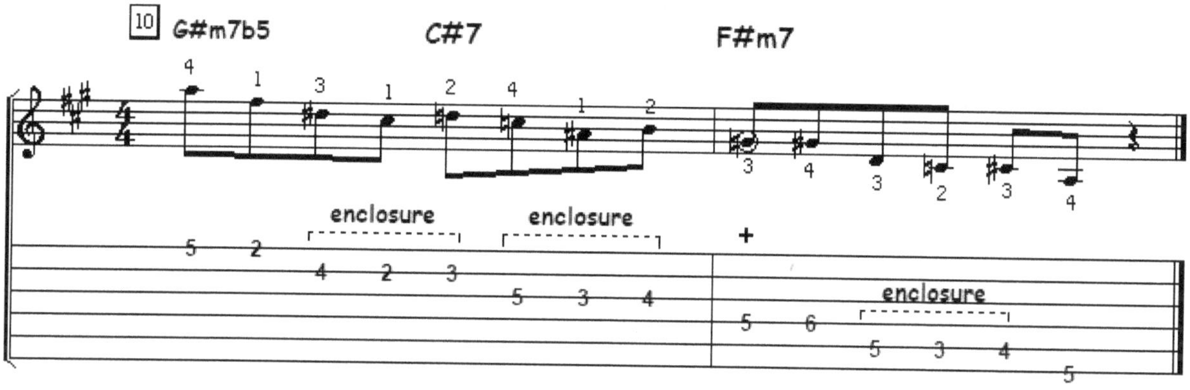
10
G#m7b5
C#7
F#m7
enclosure
enclosure
enclosure

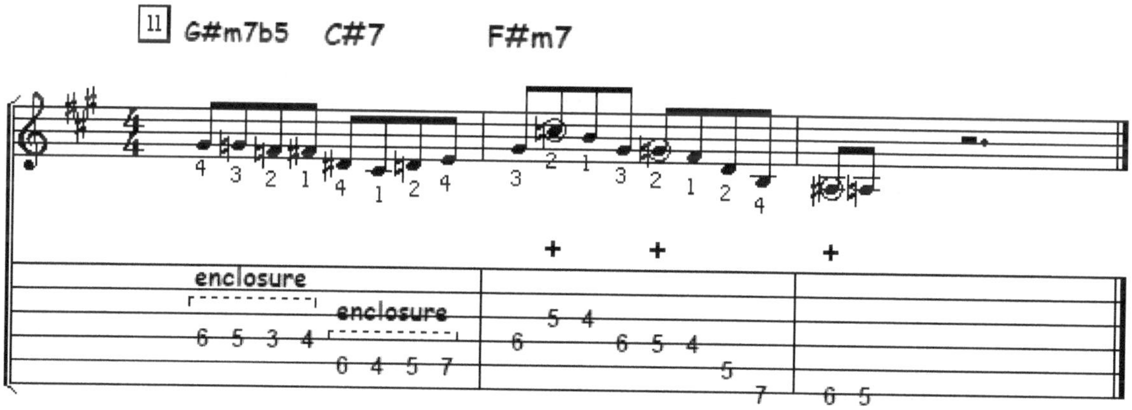
11
G#m7b5
C#7
F#m7
enclosure
enclosure

When improvising, always remember to play *from* the maps. Black and white playing is just another way of embellishing the maps, while the maps keep things melodic and make it easy to visualize resolutions and voice leading between key centers. Don't forget to play out of order and that it's okay to skip while using the fourths and your pentatonic power, even mixing in some fractions. Those concepts are the meat and potatoes of our lines and good, melodic improvisation. Use your ear and it'll guide your fingers to what sounds good. Of course, *any* guitarist who's attempting to add a jazz-fusion flavor to their playing is naturally going to become a chromaddict fast because that's the gravy right there.

Chapter Six:
Diminished Capacity

We have *one* more new master arpeggio to learn. It's a little more specialized and limited compared the more popular and widely used altered, but it's easy to memorize and use and it's very handy in a couple specific situations we might encounter in jazz standards and jazz-blues tunes.

Our new map is for the diminished sound and the great thing about it is that, using the Master Arpeggio System, we only have to remember *one* form and place it in relation to the major map we learned in the first book. The diminished sound is often associated with a couple particular chords, so it's helpful to know it so we can use it in these contexts in keeping with standard practice.

Friend or Faux?

The 7b9 chord pops up in standards every now and then and it's also a nice choice when composing or reharmonizing. It lends a particular flavor to a progression because it's voiced like a diminished chord. This is done by raising the root a half step up to the b9, so the chord becomes a *rootless voicing*. It's almost like a faux diminished chord because it's played as a diminished chord but it's a 7b9 in context. It's a nice way to get the diminished chord into a song other than using it as a passing chord.

Here's a common ii-V-I progression in A major that shows how this 7b9 chord is used with standard chord voices.

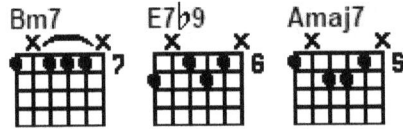

Bm7   E7♭9   Amaj7

Now let's make friends with this "faux" diminished chord and capitalize on its distinct sound. Here are our A major maps again, this time with their corresponding E half-whole diminished maps. We'll call them E in relation to the dominant sound they represent, namely the E7. It's called half-whole diminished because, playing in black and white (stepwise/scalar), there's a half step between the first two notes, which here are E and F.

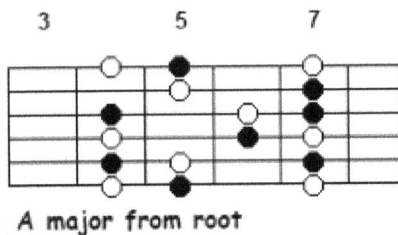

A major from root

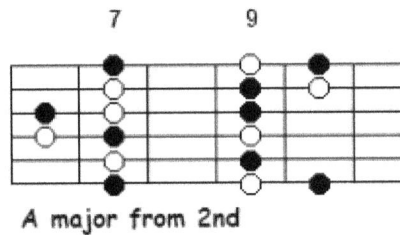

A major from 2nd

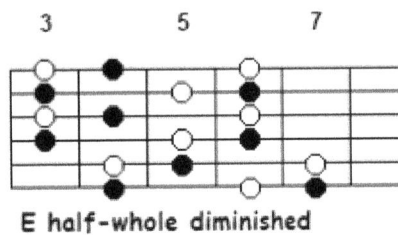

E half-whole diminished

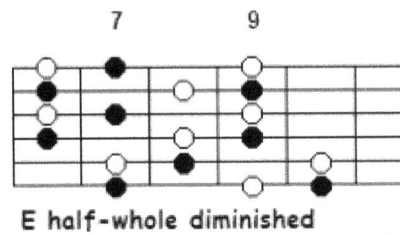

E half-whole diminished

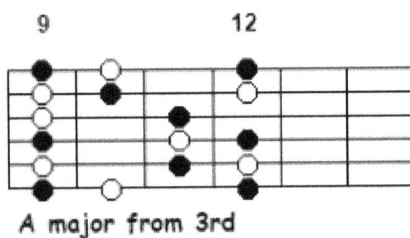

A major from 3rd

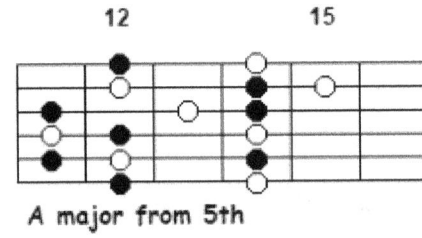

A major from 5th

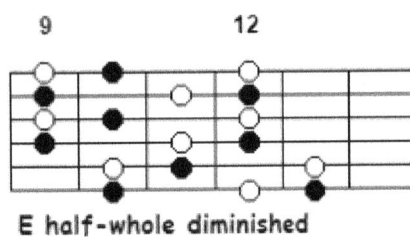

E half-whole diminished

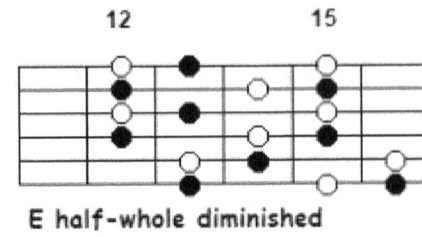

E half-whole diminished

56

A major from 6th

E half-whole diminished

The learning curve should be pretty minimal because we only have the one map to learn, so all we have to focus on is relating it to each of our major maps. Notice the *shape* of the diminished chord in the map and that'll help you place the map for improvising lines. Now let's put these in some ii-V-I lines and hear how they sound.

57

The real trick here, especially if you're coming to this from a rock or metal background, is to avoid sounding too directly diminished, like the neo-classical and shred styles. That will come with some practice and being creative with phrasing, as well as listening to jazz and looking for examples where it's used in a jazz or fusion context.

In fusion, which has a more direct link to rock, the more straight ahead diminished sound works better, but it's nice to disguise it. For either approach, we have handy tools at our disposal for mixing things up and disguising the diminished: playing out of order, skipping, fourths, and—a powerful tool—chromaticism.

A Real Sharp One . . . Well, a Sharp Four

In a jazz-blues, a common chord substitution is the #IV chord. So, in A major, we might encounter a IV7-#IV°-I7, D7-D#°-A7 in A major. Here's an example of the basic progression using some common four-note *grips*.

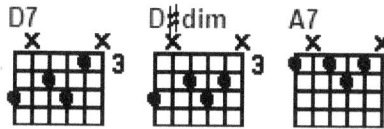

I'm just going to demonstrate this in our first position and you should be able to figure out the rest, something you'll need to do with *all* our maps when you begin learning standards and strategizing your solos and familiarizing yourself with the song form so you can improvise once it's time to throw down.

These maps are for playing over straight dominant chords with no alterations and no altered sound, which means you're playing the key center for the V chords. For D7 you would play the G major map, because G is the I chord for the key in which the D7 is the V chord and the V *pulls* toward the I. This is essentially the D Mixolydian sound. When playing *tonally*, which we're exploring here, I keep things simple and think in basic terms of major and minor, reserving *modal* thinking for playing modally and with *non-functional* harmony. Basically, go with whatever works best for you, although I'll use the key center.

We'll use the D# half-whole diminished over the D#°/#IV chord and move into the D major map over the A7 I chord. This is a more straightforward approach to this sound and it's not too *outside* sounding compared to using the altered maps.

G major (over D7)

D# dim (over D#dim)

D major (over A7)

Let's hear how this sounds in the context of some lines.

Altered States

If the context of the tune allows it—or you just want to throw more curve balls your listeners (and bandmates)—we can use the altered maps here for a decidedly more unsettled outside sound, which is always fun if you can get away with it.

In this case, we would simply use D altered over D7, D# half-whole diminished over the D#°, and A altered over the A7 (you can also revert to the D major map for a more resolved sound). Remember your pentatonics within here because they work great in this context.

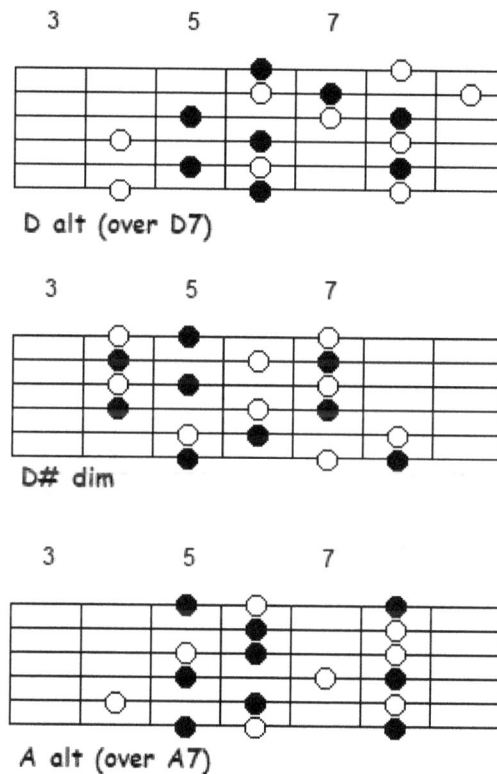

D alt (over D7)

D# dim

A alt (over A7)

Let's hear these maps used in a few lines. Notice in Example 8 the varied approach of using the direct map in the first measure, a more black & white approach in the second, and the pentatonic phrases in the last. It's a more *lyrical* approach in the phrasing and provides a nice contrast to the other approaches. Mixing things up creates a lot of variety and keeps things more interesting and less predictable.

The diminished provides some nice alternatives to always using the altered map, which could technically be played over the 7b9 and would even work over the #IV. It sounds just a little "wrong" over the #IV, but some people might think the altered sounds just plain wrong all the time. Those people usually don't listen to jazz.

The major, minor, altered, harmonic minor, and diminished maps are all the *main* sounds you're going to find in *tonal* jazz music and they'll work in fusion too, but things start to change in that context. There are other great sounds to use, but those are for another time (and book).

Essentially, tonal jazz is where you find most of your ii-V-I progressions, their related turnarounds, cycle progressions, tritone substitutions, secondary dominants (all those *other* V7 chords in the cyclic progressions), and the like. The chords frequently pass by much faster and move through key centers more often, so they're much trickier to navigate. That's why it helps to have a system in place to tackle them.

NOTE: I kept all the examples in this chapter in the same range of the fretboard so you can better examine what's going on and how I mix 'n match the various maps for slightly different results.

Chapter Seven:
Turn Around

Building lines on V-I and ii-V-I progressions is a standard introduction constructing lines and improvising over jazz progressions. Once this first step has been taken, the next logical move is to look at turnarounds.

A turnaround usually appears in the last couple bars or at the end of a bridge to create forward motion and take us "back to the top," to the head of the tune or main theme, usually returning to the I chord. It creates a *pull* back to the home key. The turnaround is used for transitions and frequently begins on the I and ends on the V7 or the bII7, the tritone sub for the V chord. In this section I continue each line back to the I chord so we can clearly hear the resolution. Otherwise, the lines can sound a little incomplete, something that always stumbled me when learning lines from other sources.

Learning to navigate a turnaround will prepare us for tackling jazz progressions in general and the principles we'll learn here will apply everywhere. We'll look at some of the most common turnarounds, a couple of ways to improvise over each of them using our maps, and then play a couple of lines using the techniques we've learned.

Strategize

So far, we've explored a variety of V-I, ii-V-I, and similar basic jazz progressions that have paired the major and altered maps, the harmonic minor and minor maps, and the diminished and major maps. Now we're going to look at a variety of turnarounds that mix the maps up a little more, which is not uncommon. Early traditional jazz may stick to more *unadorned* dominant chords, maybe adding *extensions* (9,11,13), but contemporary jazz may throw in more *alterations* (b9,#9,b5,#5), even on *non-functioning* dominant chords. At times, I will play the altered maps over unaltered dominant chords because I like the sound. As long as the lines are melodically and rhythmically strong, it usually works. That's something to experiment with.

When we encounter a chord progression in *tonal* jazz, turnaround or otherwise, we'll quickly notice that it doesn't stay directly in the key the song is written in. Instead, it moves through a variety of keys before returning to the home key. What we want to do to improvise lines over these progressions is to break them down into *key centers* and then figure out what maps we can draw our ideas from so we can practice in such a way that we'll have a good road map to follow when we navigate them. We have to get more creative and flexible when picking and pairing our maps, tailoring them to the progression. The good news is we have variety of options, some of which will work better than others for the song or for our personal style of expression.

I'm not going to go too deep into theory here. We're going to look at each turnaround and then check out two options we can use to improvise lines over them and get right down to business. There's a *lot* of information in here and this chapter (and the solos) will provide a wealth of knowledge that will help you in moving forward. For the first fourteen examples, I'll include some diagrams of the maps used to form the lines then I'll leave to you to find them yourself from there. Being able to mix and match your maps is a crucial skill you need to develop.

When pairing up and moving between maps, we do it like we've done from the outset, playing them frontward, backward, inside and out, and upside down, from any point. However, in time, this will become a very quick and easy process where we move fluidly between our maps as they weave through each other and intertwine. You'll find recurring movements of the maps through fourths, fifths, and other predictable patterns; practice your maps through these and you'll be ready to tackle almost anything that comes your way when playing standards on the bandstand.

The Turnarounds

I vi ii V:

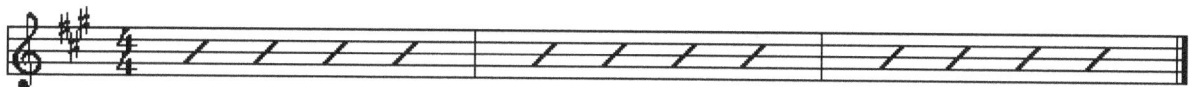

The first turnaround is very simple. It's *diatonic* and doesn't stray from the key so we can blow over the entire progression with the A major map. If we want to create more friction, however, we could use the E altered map over the second measure. A simpler way to create some tension and interest is through using our chromatic tools. Let's see how this sounds in practice.

Example 1 is a pretty straight forward question and answer style line with a passing tone in the first measure. This is very melodic and has a safer "inside" sound. In this section, I won't use anything to indicate the techniques (approach, passing, enclosure, pentatonic, etc.). You can use the diagrams to examine how I'm using them where they're included.

Example 2 two is a more scalar "black and white" line with passing tones, but notice how it's still built around a part of the master arpeggio in the first measure. I'm using the E altered map for the second measure, along with some passing tones and an approach tone, but it's still a pretty "inside" line overall and outlines a portion of the E altered map. The diagram shows the two maps the line is drawn from.

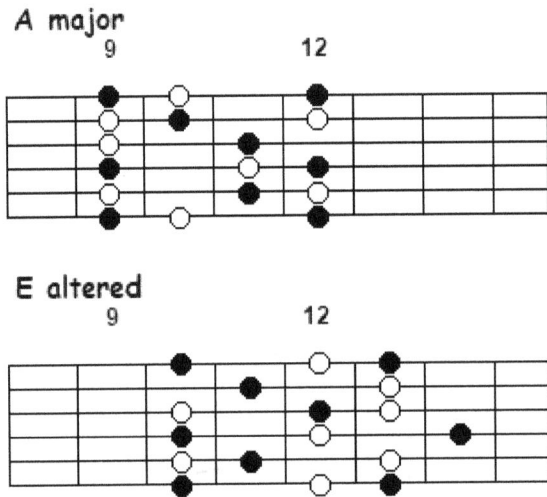

A major

E altered

I VI ii V:

Amaj7   F#7   Bm7   E7   Amaj7

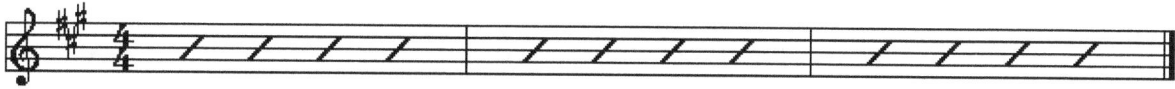

Let's look at a couple options for this turnaround.

Option 1:

- Use the A major map over the Amaj7
- B major map over the F#7 (the V of B major), creating tension as the chord and map leave the key.
- A major over the Bm7 E7 Amaj7 for our resolution.

Example 3 demonstrates Option 1 with the addition of an approach tone, passing tone, and some fourths to dress up the maps. The diagram displays the maps used for the line.

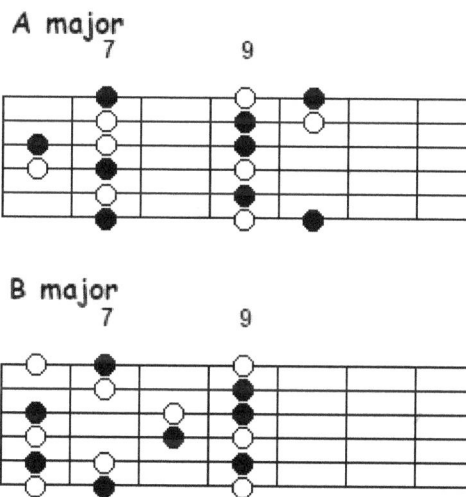

A major

B major

Option 2:

- A major over the Amaj7
- F#7 altered over F#7 (tension)
- E altered over Bm7 E7 (tension)
- A major over Amaj7 (resolution)

Example 4 shows an application of our second option and uses the pentatonics within (see first book) throughout except over the F#7, where I just use a fragment of the F# altered map.

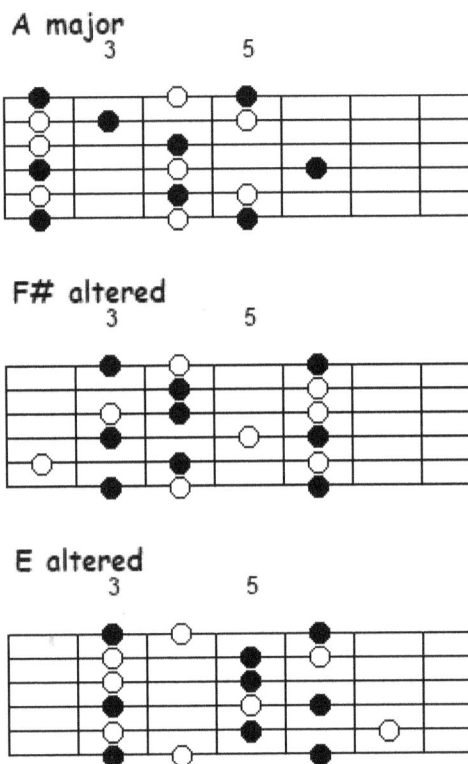

A major

F# altered

E altered

Amaj7   F#7   Bm7   E7

Amaj7

NOTE: When using the altered maps over *unaltered* 7th chords, we want to pay attention to whether or not it's appropriate for the song, especially if the 7th contains *extensions* (9th, 11th, 13th). Still, it's not *wrong* to use the altered scale; we'd simply be superimposing it4 over the 7th chord. *Superimposition* is an awesome tool to use in our playing, but it can be trickier to use in traditional jazz standards. That said, you'll sound more hip and modern, just make sure your lines make rhythmically and melodically strong statements (I can't seem to say that enough).

ALSO: These are just some options, which is part of the fun and freedom of jazz and personal taste, style, and expression. Another option, not demonstrated here, could include using the B harmonic minor over the F#7, moving to B minor over the Bm7, then switching to A major for the resolution of E7 to Amaj7. However, the E7 could be altered, calling for the altered map, or E7b9 (no root) for use with the diminished map.

71

The I chord in this turnaround could be an A7, which would call for D major map (to give it the appropriate D Mixolydian placement). Alternately, if the A7 is altered (jazz is all about mixing things up), then the A altered could be the best option. Always keep these things in mind when strategizing and preparing to improvise over a tune. Try different things out and see what tickles your ear and inspires you.

Always keep in mind that a strong melody and rhythmic line goes a long way. While just playing the wrong scale may sound awful, a strong statement can sound like something hip and superimposed if what you play next is more "inside." In fact, advanced musicians can completely superimpose other keys in spots just for cool outside sounds (listen to George Garzone and other horn and piano players or Scott Henderson). The important thing is that the lines have direction, moving toward their resolution points.

I VI II V:

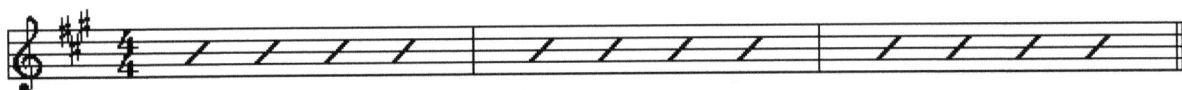

Option 1:

- B major over Amaj7 F#7 (tension)
- A major over B7 E7 Amaj7 (resolution)

Example 5 draws directly from the B major map (remember: don't be afraid to skip!) in the first measure. The second measure is taken from the pentatonics within the A major scale.

B major

7   9

A major

7   9

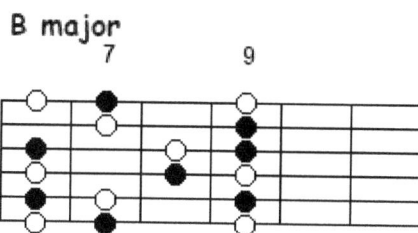

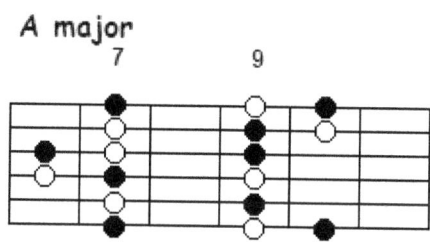

⑤ Amaj7   F#7   B7   E7   Amaj7

Option 2:

- F# altered over Amaj7 F#7 (tension)
- E altered over B7 E7 (tension)
- A major over Amaj7 (resolution)

Example 6 puts Option 2 into action by moving a melodically and rhythmically strong *motif* through the maps. These kinds of ideas really work when you're superimposing parts of the maps over a chords that are technically "wrong" (Amaj7 and B7). It works because of these factors and because it *resolves*, like the relief that comes with resolving a conflict.

F# altered

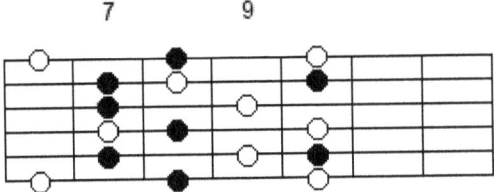

E altered

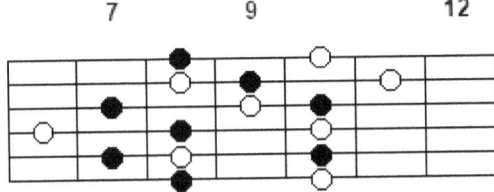

A major

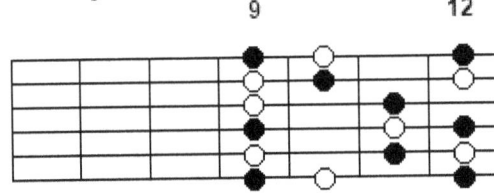

NOTE: For more options, we could play the major maps over some of the 7th chords and altered over others or even *mix* the major (Mixolydian sound) and altered maps over a single 7th chord. When we play them as black *or* white dots (straight, out of order, or skipping), we can get a nice mix of *superimposed* triads and arpeggios.

Why do I use the maps for the second chord of the measure? Because that's the chord that's usually causing the tension that will potentially resolve in the next measure. However, because we don't resolve until the Amaj7, the resolution is *suspended*—postponed—by moving along. I build the suspense by playing *through* the measures preceding the Amaj7, which is the point of resolution. I "ignore" some of the chords (often the m7) and blow over them, but the lines are strong and it all works out.

iii VI ii V:

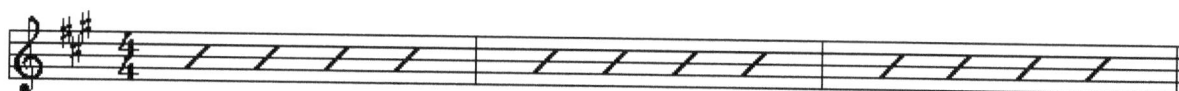

NOTE: the iii chord simply a substitute for the I chord. However, putting it before the VI7 *dominant* chord creates a *secondary* ii-V, something we always want to be watching for anywhere and everywhere in jazz progressions.

Option 1:

- B major over C#m7 and F#7 (this is a ii-V of B major)
- A major over Bm7 E7 Amaj7 (resolution)

Example 7 is a melodic line that uses some passing and approach tones. Otherwise it's a pretty straightforward melodic idea with some intervallic playing at the end. The maps are set up to help you think more intervallic than you might normally with approaching from a strictly scalar background. This can spawn a wealth of new ideas.

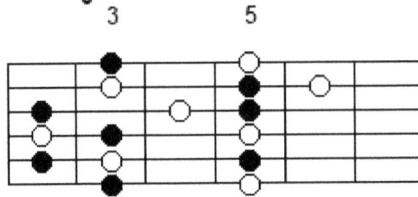

B major

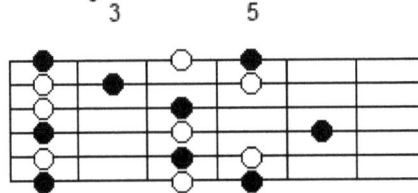

A major

Option 2:

- F# altered over C#m7 F#7 (tension)
- E altered over Bm7 E7 (tension)
- A major over Amaj7 (resolution)

Example 8 mixes the maps with approach and passing tones and some black and white playing. The first measure *superimposes* a C7 over C#m7 for an interesting outside sound just a half step away. Third measure features an enclosure. Notice how all the chromatic notes really contribute to the jazz sound.

F# altered

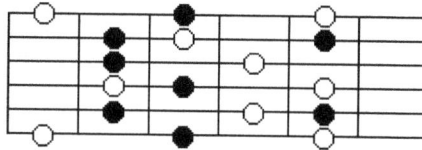

E altered

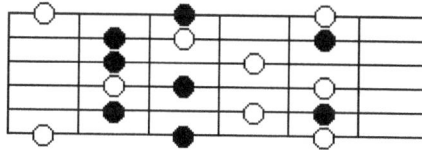

A major

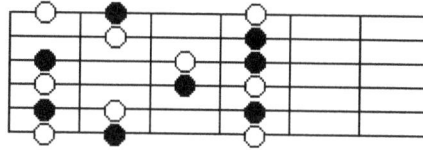

8   C#m7   F#7   Bm7   E7   Amaj7

I VI ii bII:

| Amaj7 | F#7 | Bm7 | Bb7 | Amaj7 |

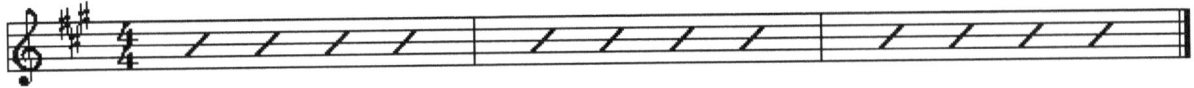

Option 1:

- B major over A maj7 F#7 (tension)
- Eb major over Bm7 Bb7 (tension)
- A major over Amaj7 (resolution)

Example 9 is pretty straightforward, using passing and approach tones to embellish triad and arpeggio portions of the map.

B major

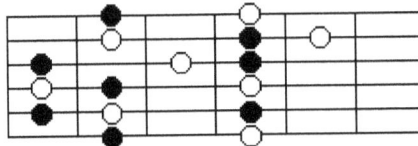

Eb major

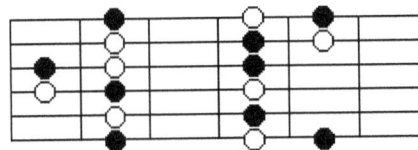

A major

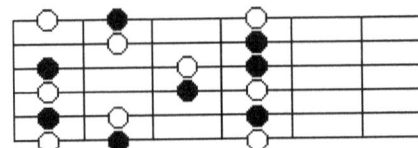

Option 2:

- F# altered over Amaj7 F#7 (tension)
- Bb altered over Bm7 Bb7 (tension)
- A major over Amaj7 (resolution)

Example 10 uses an approach tone in the second measure and some black and white scalar playing in the third measure to liven up some melodic phrases.

10 Amaj7 F#7 Bm7 Bb7 Amaj7

I #1° ii V:

Amaj7   A#°7   Bm7   E7   Amaj7

Option 1:

- A major over Amaj7
- A# diminished over A#°7 (tension)
- A major over Bm7 E7 Amaj7 (resolution)

Example 11 is very straightforward in the first measure and gets black and white with passing tones for the following.

A major

7   9

A# diminished

7   9

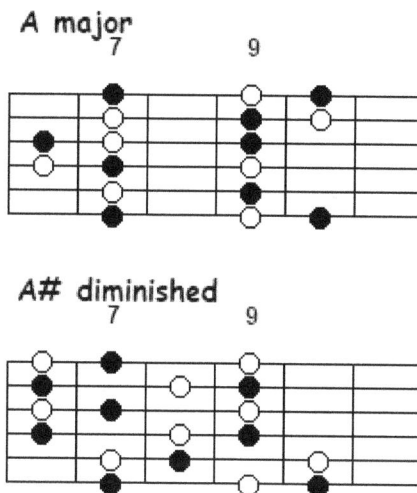

11 Amaj7 A#°7   Bm7   E7   Amaj7

Option 2:

- A# diminished over Amaj7 A#°7 (tension)
- E altered over Bm7 E7 (tension)
- A major over Amaj7 (resolution)

Example 12 is once again pretty straightforward, creating an arpeggio that skips a note to disguise the diminished sound somewhat. Notice how I use the transition from altered to major to create a sort of "new arpeggio" shape before going into a triad once again using our skipping technique to finish the line. A lot of great arpeggio sounds can be created by not only skipping notes, but also combining that with switching between black and white notes. Both traditional and more uniquely voiced arpeggios can be generated this way, as well as by combining them with fourths.

A# diminished

E altered

A major

12 | Amaj7   A#°7   Bm7   E7   Amaj7

I biii° ii V (biii diminished turnaround):

Amaj7   C°7   Bm7   E7   Amaj7

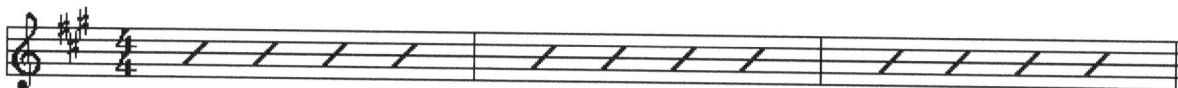

Option 1:

- A major over Amaj7
- C diminished over C°7 (tension)
- A major over Bm7 E7 Amaj7 (resolution)

Example 13 starts black and white phrase before using a straight-up portion of the diminished map, then goes out of order for the remainder of the line with the addition of a displaced passing tone. Notice the "incidental" chromaticism that's created moving between the A major and C diminished maps, which creates smooth transitions and cool sounds.

C diminished

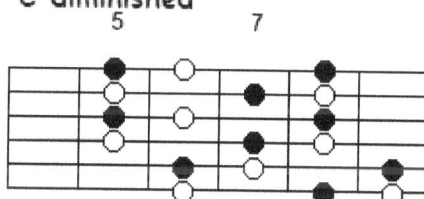

A major

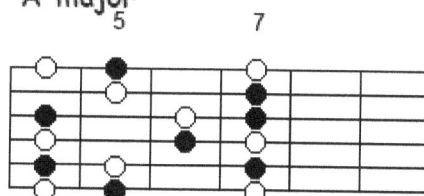

Option 2:

- C diminished over Amaj7 C°7 (tension)
- E altered over Bm7 E7 (tension)
- A major over Amaj7 (resolution

Example 14, first measure, is all partial map shapes we've seen before when skipping. We should be able to see these other options available within the diminished map. The rest of the line is derived from the pentatonics within.

C diminished

E altered

A major

[14] Amaj7   C°7   Bm7   E7

Amaj7

I vi iv bVII (hidden ii-V):

Amaj7   F#m7   Dm7   G7   Amaj7

Option 1:

- A major over Amaj7 F#m7
- C major over Dm7 G7, the ii-V of C major (tension)
- A major over Amaj7

Example 15 is an easy melodic line made up of two simple phrases that should be easy to play and understand. For delayed gratification, I let that first note of the third measure clash before resolving it. I love the sound of seconds and flat seconds when used in jazz and fusion (or elsewhere).

Option 2:

- A major over Amaj7 F#m7
- G altered over Dm7 G7 (tension)
- A major over Amaj7 (resolution)

Example 16 is full of variety and even shreds a little, pulling us more away from jazz and toward jazz-rock fusion. The first measure combines a pentatonic scale with passing and approach tones before sweeping some arpeggios in the second measure and concluding with some phrasing that again uses passing and approach tones. Chromatic notes are such a big part of the jazz and fusion sound. Also, notice how we're mixing all of our techniques more and more so that the direct maps are less and less obvious. The first measure sounds great with hybrid picking too.

16 Amaj7   F#m7   Dm7   G7

Amaj7

I bIII II bII:
Amaj7   C7   B7   Bb7   Amaj7

Option 1:

- F major over Amaj7 C7 (tension)
- Eb major over B7 Bb7 (tension)
- A major over Amaj7 (resolution)

Example 17 works with a pentatonic phrase and passing tone then goes for a portion of the map with a passing tone and finishes using the fourths.

Option 2:

- C altered over Amaj7 C7 (tension)
- Bb altered over B7 Bb7 (tension)
- A major over Amaj7 (resolution)

Example 18 is the most scalar line yet, in much more of a jazz-rock fusion sound and style. It's very black and white with a lot of passing tones. I'm still thinking and playing from the maps and just filling "holes" with passing tones. It's the opposite of how we traditionally think: scales with triads and arpeggios within. Instead, we think of master arpeggios that we can play any portion of in various ways and contain scales within.

18 Amaj7   C7   B7   Bb7

Amaj7

I bIII bVI bII:

          Amaj7   C7   F#7   Bb7   Amaj7

Option 1:

- F major over Amaj7 C7 (tension)
- Eb major over F#7 Bb7 (tension)
- A major over Amaj7 (resolution)

89

Example 19 keeps things simple and uses the pentatonics within the maps along with some passing and approach tones for a nice melodic treatment to this progression.

Option 2:

- C altered over Amaj7 C7 (tension)
- E altered over F#7 E7 (tension)
- A major over Amaj7 (resolution)

Example 20 just picks a path through the map (use your ears and let your fingers follow) and then follows with very simple, melodic phrases.

Chapter Eight: Solo Flight

This is the climax we've been building up to. It's time to apply our major, minor, altered, harmonic minor, and diminished maps to a jazz blues solo in A major. I'm using chord progressions that will apply *all* of our maps so we get to use everything and hear it all in a real working context.

I will indicate which maps I'm using and the various techniques where there's space. Chromatic passing and approach tones will be circled and marked with a plus (+) sign.

I've labeled the enclosures and side-slipping, but you should be able to see where I use the pentatonic scales within the master arpeggios. I leave it to you to see the arpeggio positions and the pentatonic scales I extract from them, as well as the triads and arpeggios I use, including playing them out of order, skipping a note, using quartal ideas, and the 3/4 and 4/3 inversions. They're pretty much all in there.

I don't specifically think about *what* I'm playing in great detail, instead focusing on my phrasing and creating nice flowing, melodic lines. I'm not thinking about *exactly* what chord tones, extensions or alterations I'm playing because they all work if I'm in key. What's not a chord tone is *always* an extension or alteration. If not, it's a chromatic note and your ear will quickly inform you if you're using it correctly (but remember: if it *sounds* good, it *is* good).

Notice where the phrases are contained within a measure and where they span two or three measures, how the ideas and maps connect (sometimes a single line moves through more than one map), and some of the recurring ideas I use as the "glue" to hold things together. I frequently begin and end

91

lines on upbeats—something I feel lends to a jazzy feel—and I swing my eighth notes.

Notice where the phrases are contained within a measure and where they span two or three measures, how the ideas and maps connect (sometimes a single line moves through more than one map), and some of the recurring ideas I use as the "glue" to hold things together. I frequently begin and end lines on upbeats—something I feel lends to a jazzy feel—and I swing my eighth notes.

I will also indicate how I personally finger the notes as I've been doing all along. You may be comfortable using your own fingerings, but these are just ways I frequently use to set myself up for moving between positions, which I've developed by carefully watching what some of the guitarists I admire are doing in similar playing situations. I frequently use sweep picking, economy picking, hybrid picking, and fingerpicking wherever it's most comfortable for me to play a line. I encourage you to use the techniques that you find easiest or experiment with them if you're expanding your techniques.

Strategize

Often, when learning a jazz tune, you will come across a *lead sheet* or a *chord chart*. Below is a chord chart for a basic 12-bar jazz blues in A major. It's important that you understand chord progressions and how to analyze them so you can learn and study the piece and come up with soloing strategies you can practice while you learn the song's form and get comfortable with soloing over the chord progressions.

A7   D7   Ab7   A7sus   A7   Em7   A7

D7   D#°7   A7sus   A7   C#m7b5   F#7

Bm7   E7   A7   F#7   Bm7   E7

Below is the same chord chart where I've chosen the most obvious options I have for improvising lines over the progressions. The *general* rule of thumb is, you can use the altered master arpeggio over a dominant chord if it's just a straight-up dominant with no extensions, (9,11,13) because the only "clashing" note is the 5th, a very flexible and optional note to use in a chord voicing. I use a lot of *shell* voices and grips derived from the shells, which often don't contain the 5th. However, the altered usually works even when the 5th is present.

If any of the extensions are present, it's "safest" to use the associated major map. So, for A7, D major is the map of choice because A7 is the V of D major and therein lies the D Mixolydian. This rule of thumb is not a hard and fast rule and throughout this book I've played the altered maps over an unaltered dominant 7th. It's all about context, flow, keeping your ideas melodically and rhythmically strong and grounded, and knowing where you're going, i.e. playing *toward* points of resolution or the conclusion of a strong idea. Make strong musical statements.

If the dominant chord is altered (b9,#9,b5,#5), the altered scale is most often the strongest choice and will best complement the harmony in creating dissonance and moving toward a point of resolution or the next idea. Although we've been playing over V-I and ii-V-I progressions in major and minor, many real life situations feature *non-functioning* (unresolving) dominant chords moving in *cycles*, *tri-tone substitutions* or other variations on progressions. So it's important to learn how to move the major and altered maps in fourths and chromatically because you'll encounter them frequently.

In the eighth measure where we play the B harmonic minor, we can resolve that into the B minor, but because the Bm7 is the ii chord of the song's key of A major, it's best to switch to the A major map (B Dorian, *modally*) while soloing to help move us harmonically toward E7, the V chord.

Personally, I tend to play the map for the second chord in each measure. For example, I use the Db major or Ab altered for D7 – Ab7 in the second measure of the jazz-blues, because the Ab altered will frequently work over either the Ab7 or its altered form and it's the V of Db major, so the Ab Mixolydian sound over an unaltered Db7 chord. In fact, if you want to be *really* creative, you can mix the Ab major and Db altered maps over that measure for some very interesting lines. Ultimately, *rules* are more suggestions and there are many jazz artists who break them. Just blowing over some chords is by far not a unique or innovative technique in jazz just don't ignore the important ones. So, alternately, you could pick a map for the first chord of each measure or for *each* chord of every measure, but that's *way* too much thinking even if it's the most "theoretically" correct thing to do.

It might be helpful to print a copy or your lead sheet and a pen or pencil (or you can do it all in a program and print it out) and analyze the piece of music and the roles the chords are playing then choose the most obvious maps you'll use to play over them. You'll want to figure out where you may encounter unaltered and altered dominants and take that into consideration. Armed with this information, you're ready to develop a game plan and practice improvising lines over the form. I tend to use a looper and start with a bar or chord at a time when first starting out, moving up to two to four measures and, eventually the entire twelve bars until you're comfortable.

Line 1:
| A7 | | D7 | Ab7 | A7sus | A7 | Em7 | A7 |
| I | | IV | (bII7) | I | | | (ii V) |

D major / A altered — Db major / Ab altered — D major / A altered — D major / A altered

Line 2:
| D7 | | D#°7 | | A7sus | A7 | C#m7b5 | F#7 |
| IV | | #IV° | | I | | | (ii V) |

G major / D altered — D# diminished — D major / A altered — B harmonic minor

Line 3:
| Bm7 | | E7 | | A7 | F#7 | Bm7 | E7 |
| ii | | V7 | | I | VI7 | | (ii V) |

B minor / A major — A major / E altered — C# major / F# altered — A major / E altered

An important thing to remember is that, when improvising, *no* jazz musician (unless it's *free jazz*) is up there playing things they've *never* played at least once or twice (if not much more) in private. No one puts their neck completely on the line unless they're a new student that has just picked up their instrument recently. Improvised solos are the execution of many ideas that have been explored before. When practicing, you learn what works and what doesn't, what things are comfortable and fall under your fingers nicely, what sounds and phrases you like, and you draw on all of this when it comes time to take a solo. Improvised solos are the result of much discipline ... and trial and error while learning a piece of music. When it comes time to solo, you've worked out all the kinks.

Solo on a Jazz-Blues in A major

Following is a 24-bar solo on a 12-bar jazz blues in A major. For the first time through the progression, I just play a simple rhythm using only *guide tones*, namely the 3rd and the 7th, except for the A7sus, where I avoid the 3rd until I play the guide tones for the A7. When just playing the guide tones, the rhythm is open enough where I could use either of the associated major or altered maps . . . or *both*. I stick to the major maps for most measures except for the E7 just before the turnaround, just to keep things harmonically interesting after using the A major map over the Bm7 in the previous measure.

For the second time through the jazz blues (measures 13-24) I use more *harmonically dense* (dissonant) voices and so I go for the altered sounds more because they complement the harmony and progression better. I've labeled which maps I'm using so you can better see how I'm applying them in context. Also, through the span of 24 bars, we get to see just about everything we've explored applied in a working situation and hear the variations in the process.

Let's get to it . . .

Page deliberately left blank

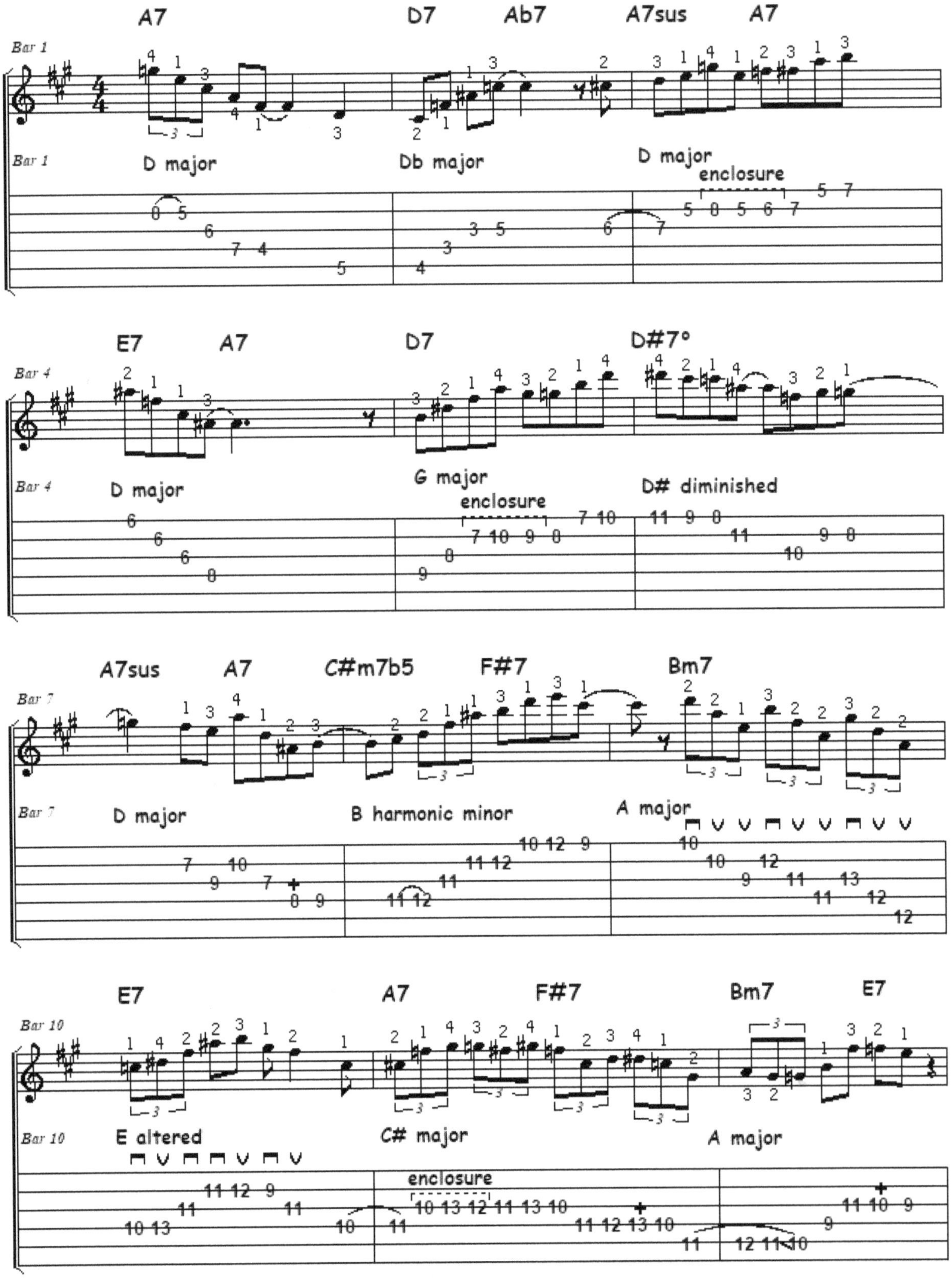
A7 D7 Ab7 A7sus A7
Bar 1
Bar 1
D major
Db major
D major
enclosure
E7 A7 D7 D#7°
Bar 4
Bar 4
D major
G major
enclosure
D# diminished
A7sus A7 C#m7b5 F#7 Bm7
Bar 7
Bar 7
D major
B harmonic minor
A major
E7 A7 F#7 Bm7 E7
Bar 10
Bar 10
E altered
C# major
enclosure
A major

A7 E7 D7 A7sus A7
Bar 13
E altered
Ab altered
A major
E7 A7 D7 D#7°
Bar 16
A altered
D altered
D diminished
A7sus A7 C#m7b5 F#7 Bm7
Bar 19
A major
B harmonic minor
A major
side-slip
E7 A7 F#7 Bm7 E7
Bar 22
E altered
F# altered
E altered

In Conclusion

Notice where and how I use melodic and rhythmic *motifs*. They're the glue that holds the solo together, tying one line to another, creating a flow. *Call and response* lines are another valuable tool I use to keep the continuity when connecting ideas. Practicing connecting the master arpeggios helps to create lines that move through the maps fluidly. So when I'm using more "black and white" scalar lines that move through the changes, the maps help me to navigate easily, showing me where to go so I don't get lost.

Another important thing to notice is that I don't jump all over the place even though I cover much of the fretboard throughout the duration of the 24 bars. Instead, I often connect my lines with a note that's only a half step away from one I just played or I even start a new line on a shared note that's common to both maps. When I move to another area on the fretboard, it's musically strategic, bringing me to a place where I will develop my next set of ideas.

The thing to always keep in mind is, like any good solo, you want to tell a story rather than just ramble on. Use the full range of the neck to do that in a way that keeps your listeners engaged. Another very valuable skill to develop is to improvise on the melody (or head) of the tune by altering it rhythmically and embellishing it in various ways, such as with chromaticism. This will tie your solo in to the overall musical theme. An absolute master at this approach was Thelonious Monk, a personal favorite.

Being able to analyze and understand the chord progressions and key changes of traditional jazz is one area that requires some attention. It's important to understand the relationship between the master arpeggios and the key centers and to *always* be musical and creative, melodic and rhythmic, and to be able to mix and match the maps according to the song form and progressions. With these valuable skills, you'll be ready for anything that comes your way. Remember, music is expression, so express yourself!

Afterword

I hope that MAS4JI II helps you to up your game and take things to the next level with your creativity. This method was, first and foremost, the answer to my own questions and the way over and around my own obstacles to improvising and creating endless lines and solos in the moment without too much overthinking. I hope that this method helps you and opens the doors to new levels of creativity and expands your playing into new territory.

The next book, **The Master Arpeggio System for Jazz Improvisation III: Far Out,** will kick things up a notch or three as we reach for *sonic freedom* and move from more traditional jazz-blues forms into the realm of modal jazz and fusion to explore some very modern concepts that will take us further outside while still keeping us grounded. This will be contain advanced studies that will take our playing to new levels of creativity and expression. We'll even get a little *atonal* and more avant-garde along the way as we push the limits of everything we've learned so far.

About the Author

About the Author: Dennis Roberts started his musical journey in his mid-teens as a self-taught guitarist playing hard rock and heavy metal, but was always very interested in studying music theory and playing techniques. It wasn't until his mid-30s that he went to college and formally studied music theory, performance, and recording in a stimulating academic atmosphere. While delving into some basic classical Dennis kept focusing mainly on jazz, a style he's been listening to since childhood. Dennis graduated with honors and continues to pursue his music passions.